Department of Education and Science

Education 5 to 9

An illustrative survey of 80 first schools in England

London
Her Majesty's Stationery Office

No assumption can be made about government commitment to the provision of additional resources as a result of this report.

ISBN 0 11 270530 8

Contents

Preface

The preliminary work for this survey of 80 first schools, all established as first schools for at least three years, was undertaken in 1977. Visiting the selected sample began a year later and was completed in 1979. The findings of this survey relate, therefore, to the circumstances of that time.

Since then, various developments may have affected first schools generally and therefore some of those in the survey. Sharply falling rolls, or a changed pattern in the distribution of resources for education may have led to a decreased purchasing power. Some recent policy developments and initiatives, too, may well have had their effect, whether through the increased awareness of the need for multicultural aspects of education to loom larger or the new role of schools in the way in which children's special needs are met or through the enhanced position of governors in a school's life.

Such changes reflect only the constant adjustments that a dynamic education service has to offer. The relevance of this survey is not only to teachers and children in first schools, but also to all those concerned in the education of 5 to 9 year olds.

This survey could not have been carried out without the cooperation of the many heads, teachers and ancillary staff involved. We are particularly indebted to those schools which allowed us to use samples of children's work (and to the children who produced it).

1   Introduction

1.1 Two main issues led to the formation of first schools. One was raised by the Central Advisory Committee under the chairmanship of Lady Plowden, which, in its report[1] noted that summer-born children, many of whom had only two years or two years and one term in infant schools, did less well on average than children who, because they were born earlier in the year, had a longer first stage of schooling. The Committee also took the view that 7 year old children on the brink of learning to read would do better if kept in an extended infants school than if transferred to a junior school; and that an extension for 11 to 12 year olds of the methods used in primary schools would be to their advantage. The Committee proposed: nursery education for all whose parents wished it; first schools for children from 5 to 8 years; and middle schools for 8 to 12 year olds. The other issue concerned changes in secondary schools. In the mid 1960s local education authorities were preparing for school leaving age to be raised and at the same time many of them were proposing to establish comprehensive schools in the whole or part of their areas. They wished to avoid undue increases in the number of year groups and changes in the sizes of their secondary schools (not least so that efficient use could be made of their existing stock of school buildings) — delaying the age of transfer from primary schools could help towards achieving these aims which would also lead to a longer period of pre-secondary schooling, opening the way to implementing the Central Advisory Committee's proposals.

1.2 The 1964 Education Act made it possible to vary the age of transfer of pupils from one stage of schooling to the next. It became legal, therefore, to establish schools with pupils of both primary and secondary age on their rolls — middle schools — and so open the way for the formation of first schools. By January 1975 there were 2,093 first schools spread among 48 LEAs (Table 1). Of these 828 were for 5 to 8 year olds and 1,128 for 5 to 9 year olds; the rest of the first schools catered for 5 to 7 or 5 to 10 year olds. By January 1978 the total number of first schools had reached 2,706, and 2,887 by January 1980 (Table 2). There are also some 387 first schools combined with middle schools. These were not included in the list from which the sample for this survey was drawn.

---

[1] *Children and their primary schools.* A report of the Central Advisory Council for Education (England). Chairman: Lady Plowden, JP. HMSO

1.3 The survey which took place between Easter 1978 and July 1979 is based on inspections of 33 5 to 8 and 47 5 to 9 schools all of which had been in operation as first schools for at least three years; the number of 5 to 8 compared to that of 5 to 9 schools in the survey reflects the national proportions of these two types. This report differs in a number of ways from the HMI Report on Primary Education published in 1978[1] and was designed to include more description of children's work and, because it is based on a smaller sample, makes less use of statistics.

1.4 Information was collected about the organisation and staffing in the schools (cf Appendix I), but the main weight of evidence was in the form of narrative descriptions of the work of the children. HMI observed the full range of teaching provided by the schools and assessed the work and achievements in terms of appropriateness for the children's ages and abilities. The descriptions show what is achieved by young children when conditions are especially conducive to learning. They are included partly to illustrate points made in the report, and so that readers may share to some degree the advantages that HMI had in observing the teachers and children at work.

1.5 Taking the schools as a whole, a number of typical features was found. No one school will necessarily contain all of them. The paragraphs which follow (1.6 to 1.14) make generalisations about the most common features.

1.6 A first school takes great care in and devotes much effort to introducing children and their parents to their first days in school. Before admission, children and their parents are encouraged to visit the school and spend some time taking part in an activity such as painting or listening to stories. As their children go through the school, parents are invited to see their work and discuss their progress with the teacher. Children learn to live harmoniously in a community, to begin to accept responsibility, to show concern for others, to care for their own and other people's possessions. The stability and encouragement provided by the staff help the children to gain self-confidence and to develop a positive attitude to their work.

1.7 Reading, writing and mathematics are given priority, and often children use these skills to further their learning, though by the time they are eight or nine they may be insufficiently challenged and produce work, especially in reading and writing, which does not always match their ability.

1.8 The wide range of work across the curriculum gives opportunities for learning about people and the physical world. Children enjoy music, experiment with a variety of materials, learn to use tools and engage in physical activity. They are helped to acquire essential skills, knowledge and ideas through working from first-hand experiences relating to their interests and their surroundings, supported by books and other materials. Children work with enthusiasm and respond with excitement and satisfaction as they acquire new skills and make

---

[1] *Primary education in England.* A survey by HM Inspectors of Schools. HMSO 1978

discoveries. Teaching resources available to help these processes in the schools are not always used to the full.

1.9 The head if not in first headship has previously been head of an infant or primary school. The thinking, planning and organisation within the school are, naturally, affected by the previous experience of the head whose job it is to provide leadership for the staff and to be responsible for overall decisions about the pattern of organisation and the level of work. The teachers, the majority of whom are women, are usually responsible for all the work of their own classes, though sometimes they receive support and help from colleagues for certain parts of the curriculum, such as music. Each child's individuality is recognised in that work is planned to take account of it; children also gain stimulus from working some of the time in groups or as a class. Special group tuition is often provided for the less able children, usually in the form of extra help with reading. Teachers are concerned to let all children know that their work is valued.

1.10 Classes of mixed age (arising either from choice or necessity) provide a certain continuity; however, at the same time, teachers encounter difficulty in catering for a wide age range and an even greater ability range. In some of these classes the needs of the children at the extremes of the age and ability ranges are not fully met.

1.11 Paid ancillary help is usually available to assist the staff in a variety of ways, in and out of the classroom, and particularly with the youngest children. Ancillaries prepare materials or help individual children in their practical work; assistance of this kind is occasionally provided voluntarily by parents as well.

1.12 The premises, which if not purpose-built housed a primary school prior to reorganisation, are well maintained. Teachers make them attractive and interesting and they contain displays of children's work, pictures and charts, natural objects, plants and flowers. School sites are planted with shrubs and trees, gardens and lawns and there are opportunities for the children to engage in such activities as games, gardening and imaginative play.

1.13 Like all schools, the first school exhibits strengths and weaknesses. Although the leadership of the head determines the quality of the education throughout the school, the strengths and enthusiasm of individual teachers affect positively the work of a particular part of the curriculum, or the work of a particular class.

1.14 Although the survey made possible this general and fairly typical picture, provision and practices within individual schools and between them were as varied as in most phases of English education. Appendix I sets out the details of, and the text itself illustrates, these differences.

2   The work of the schools

2.1 Normally some parts of the school day or week were set aside for work that concentrated on a particular part of the curriculum: learning to read and write, mathematics, music or physical education. A substantial part of the work could not neatly be categorised under discrete subject headings. For example the preparation and use of a class shop engaged children in the use of skills in constructing the shop and making the contents; in preparing posters and price lists; in weighing, measuring and learning about money; and in role play, developing language and practising social skills. However, what children learn from activities such as these provides the essential foundations for the study of separate subjects which begin to be more easily identifiable in the later years of their first school education. It was no surprise that the school day was more likely to be divided according to activity than by subject, or that skills and knowledge acquired in one area of the curriculum were used in another.

2.2 One such activity included nature study and work in language, mathematics and art. A disused railway cutting adjoining one school had been cleared in the recent past by staff and children and named Nature Valley by the children. Within this area a nature trail had been established by the 8 and 9 year olds with the help of the staff. During the visits to the cutting the younger children were encouraged to observe and to listen carefully; paying due regard to the conservation of species, specimens were taken back to the classrooms where more thorough discussion took place. The older children plotted the location of the trees and wild flowers on a plan of the cutting; trees, other plants and animals were classified. The cycle of natural events and the pattern of growth and regeneration were observed and recorded. Samples of leaf, twig and bark brought into the classroom were identified with the help of good quality reference books, descriptions of the trees were written and drawings, diagrams and graphs were made. Work done on the surface area of leaves and the ordering of leaves by size led the children to make written observations about the variability in the size of leaves from the same tree, and the variety of size of leaves from different tree species. They carefully identified wild flowers, using books and charts and made accurate and sensitive drawings of the flowers. This experience helped the children to develop a concern for living things and the plants and animals in the class-room were well cared for; thorough attention was paid to watering, feeding and cleanliness.

LANGUAGE AND LITERACY — READING

The approach to reading

2.3 The teaching of reading was regarded as having the highest of priorities in virtually all of the schools. Almost without exception the teachers recognised the importance of spoken language as an essential foundation for learning to read and write and provided many opportunities for the children to express themselves orally. In approximately three-quarters of the schools the level of attainment of most children in early reading skills was satisfactory in relation to their age and ability, but in most of these schools these skills could have been further developed with the older children. In twelve schools, where the children were thoroughly taught, and the provision was good, many of them achieved a high standard quickly and were fluent readers by the age of seven. Children were introduced to books from the age of five years and in the most successful schools there was a combination of look-and-say and phonic methods; reading practice was given a high priority. Phonics were thoroughly and systematically taught at an appropriate stage; the children learned the sounds of letters and groups of letters in order to read words that were new to them. However, in many schools there was an unduly prolonged concentration on the basic reading scheme, especially for the able readers who should have been extending their skills while reading more demanding books of reference and fiction. Almost all the schools lacked guidelines on the extension and development of reading skills.

2.4 In almost all schools the youngest children were introduced too quickly to published reading schemes and phonic practice, with the result that some were confused and made little progress. The children spent a good deal of time decoding print with the result that they read mechanically and with little understanding of, or interest in, the content. In a few schools the reading programme itself was poorly planned: the objectives of the early stages of reading had not been worked out; the children made a slow start and proceeded at too leisurely a pace for interest to be maintained or a sense of achievement experienced.

2.5 In a minority of schools the older children were encouraged to use books for finding answers to their questions in connection with topics and displays, in order to extract information and compare ideas. This they did effectively, though it was rare to find good practice consistently throughout a school. Intervention by the teachers drew attention to appropriate books where children could find additional information. In other schools, even where the supply was reasonable, reference books were frequently under-used. Books were often used only for casual browsing and not for the development of skills necessary for the seeking and collecting of information. Few instances were seen of children becoming engrossed in books, fiction or non-fiction, but in the small number of schools where this did occur, it clearly reflected the opportunities given to them and the time they had to pursue reading for pleasure.

Supplementary provision

2.6 Additional help was provided in approximately two-thirds of the schools, mainly for older children who found learning to read difficult. The work was usually done with individuals or with small groups and on a regular basis by withdrawal from the class. The children made good progress when the work was closely linked with and supported their classroom activities, and when the class-teacher was involved in the remedial work. Separate teaching for the very able was provided for 94 children, usually among the oldest, in 11 schools. The work consisted mainly of reading and general English.

Use of resources for early reading

2.7 There were wide variations in both the quantity and the quality of materials used for early reading practice. Most schools used a number of suitable schemes and had some system of linking books of approximately the same level, thus providing a wider vocabulary and a greater variety of reading material than a single scheme includes. Overall a fifth of the schools relied on a single reading scheme; this was more likely to be true in the 5 to 8 schools, though these schools usually had a good supply of supplementary readers.

2.8 Reading material related to the children's interests provided the motivation for some children to learn to read. Books made by the teachers provided a valuable source of early reading material and were used in approximately a fifth of the schools. Where the books were based on the children's current interests and topics and the language used was linked with their spoken vocabulary, the children's incentive to read and their enjoyment were increased. The first introduction to reading for a group of 5 year olds, for example, was through a book made by the teacher about gerbils kept by the children. In another class the children showed sustained interest in the teacher's captions attached to pictures recording their visit to a dairy farm. For many children individual and class news books provided a further source of reading material, as did collections of the children's stories and, less often, poems and prayers.

2.9 Apparatus and cards were used, often extensively, in two-thirds of the 5 to 8 schools and in a quarter of the 5 to 9 schools. Some of the material were related to the reading schemes; other materials were for sentence making, word building and analysis, word and picture matching and reading games. Reading and writing cards, story and question cards and mathematics cards requiring reading were in use in some classes.

The provision of books other than reading schemes

2.10 At the time of the survey in some two-thirds of schools both the quantity and quality of the fiction and non-fiction books were adequate or good, any deficiency tending to relate to quantity rather than quality. In about a third of the schools both the number and quality of the books were poor. In rather less than half of the schools there was a satisfactory provision of books for different areas of the curriculum. The deficiencies in 12 schools were considered to be serious. In these schools the lack of variety of books of quality and the narrow range of books containing information curtailed the children's reading for pleasure, and inhibited their learning in most areas of the curriculum. In both the 5 to 8 schools and the 5 to 9 schools shortages were most noticeable in geography and history, but they also affected other aspects of the curriculum including science, literature (including poetry) and art.

Book corners and libraries

2.11 Where they were provided, as was the case in almost all schools, the book corners in the classrooms of the 5 and 6 year olds were usually inviting and comfortable areas, with carpets, cushions and appropriate furniture; the picture and story books were suitable and attractive. In addition some classes had collections of books either within or immediately outside the classroom.

2.12 The practice of using the school library and classroom books to provide early reading material varied considerably from school to school, but in only a minority of schools were they used as an additional resource to add breadth of interest in the early stages of children's reading development. In nineteen of the schools the children were encouraged to use the class book corner and the school library from an early age, but unfortunately a sharp distinction was often made between these books and books in the reading scheme; library books were seldom used to extend the range of early reading.

2.13 At least some pupils were allowed to borrow books to take home in approximately three-fifths of the schools and over half the children who were allowed to borrow books did so. In approximately a quarter of the 5 to 8 schools and half of the 5 to 9 schools pupils could borrow books from both the school library often including those on loan from the local authority library service, and from the reading scheme. The usual pattern was for library books to be made available to older children only after they had reached a predetermined level of proficiency in reading. Sadly it was exceptional to find active encouragement for children to borrow both library books and other books from the age of 5. Overall the extent of borrowing was not good and most schools placed too much restriction on the types of books which could be borrowed, or the ages of the children who could borrow them, or both.

2.14 The degree of help given to children in selecting their school or local authority library books varied considerably. In a small number of schools the children were helped in the choice of their books by the teachers and occasionally by parents and welfare assistants; in most schools the children made their choice unaided. In a few schools there was a general enthusiasm for books and children looked forward to the weekly changing of books from the school or county library. The books were readily accessible, well catalogued and displayed in attractive and comfortable surroundings. The staff were constantly looking for ways of introducing pupils to a wider range of books and the older children sometimes wrote about the books they read. Some teachers made a point of discussing the library books with the children, either during the reading or at its conclusion, but there were classes where no discussion took place, even of the books in the reading scheme which formed the total reading experience for some children.

2.15 In approximately half of the schools the teachers communicated their enjoyment of books to the children through the enthusiasm with which they shared their own favourite poems and stories. Where books gave pleasure to the adults and the children saw the staff making good use of them, not only for stories and during class lessons, but as parts of displays and interesting collections, the children showed a similar interest in books. Enjoyment of and enthusiasm for reading were further increased in schools where the children had ample opportunity for browsing and reading, but in three-quarters of the schools such opportunities were limited. Unfortunately children's reading of stories was often not part of the planned daily programe; in general, it was seen to be an activity which children might enjoy once the set tasks had been accomplished. The children who worked more slowly might be deprived of this experience. In a small number of schools there were talks to parents on children's literature and parents were advised to encourage children to read at home. In almost half of the schools a scheme was operated which enabled children to buy books. Although many of these books were of high quality, some were not; care needs to be taken that books made available in this way are of a uniformly high standard.

LANGUAGE AND LITERACY — WRITING

The early stages

2.16 It was normal and appropriate for all children to write something every day. For most of the younger children, learning to write began with copying or tracing over captions written by teachers and relating to the children's 'news' pictures; the words and sentences were often suggested by the children. Other writing of the 5 and 6 year olds was based on topics studied by the whole class and pictures and writing were collected into class books with titles such as *The bird table* or *The cleverest things we can do.* The writing of simple stories, factual recording and some descriptive writing began to emerge at this age, and most children achieved a reasonable standard.

Different kinds of writing

2.17 As children developed they were introduced to different kinds of writing; the emphasis that schools gave to one kind or another varied. Some concentrated on factual writing linked with other areas of the curriculum such as science, or, for example, the writing of recipes after cooking; some on personal writing in diaries, letters to parents, and items for class newspapers. Others gave more attention to imaginative writing though there was little evidence of the writing of poetry. There was a good deal of story writing and the retelling of stories; a number of older children kept worthwhile records with comments on the books they had read.

2.18 Accurate recording of scientific experiments was included on topics such as 'Flight' and 'Air'; eye witness accounts of the growth and movement of tadpoles were written in some schools. Some of the older children compiled individual books on topics such as 'Detectives' and 'Transport'. A number of good examples of children's writing were collected to illustrate the variety of subjects dealt with by children. After seeing a weighbridge in use a 7 year old wrote this accurate factual account which included some mathematics:

'A weighbridge is a metal platform that lorries go over. The lorries stop and get weighed by a scale. It shows on a gauge in the wall. The gauge has numbers and a pointer. A lorry comes on with grain. Weigh it empty first and then full. Find out how much the grain weighs. Answer: 2 tons empty. 10 tons full. 8 tons of grain.'

2.19 Much of the personal writing arose from children's first hand experience. After a walk a 6 year old wrote:

'Yesterday we went for a spring walk in a place called The Lodge. When we were in the Lodge I saw a hole in a tree and I thought it was an owl hole. After that I saw some moss on a fallen down tree. When a tree has fallen down, moss grows on it and then it rots away into the ground and it is very good for growing things in. It makes the ground very rich.'

2.20 Recalling past sensory experiences an 8 year old boy wrote:

'I don't like the smell of the pigs at my uncle's farm. They stink. I don't like the smell when the grass has been mown and I hate the smell of lead pencils especially when they are new out of the box. I like the smell of new books and the smell of the baker's shop because it is a delicious smell. I don't like the smell of burning rubbish in dustbins.'

2.21 Teachers often gave children the opportunity to write in an imaginative way after providing a range of appropriate stimuli.

A class of older children listened to the story and music of *The thieving magpie;* after making collages of imaginary birds an 8 year old boy wrote the following story about his bird:

'My bird's name is Fred. Red, orange and green are his main colours. He's had a lot of battles and has never lost one. One day he was flying around the treetop and he met another bird. It was dull or it looked dull but it could do very beautiful things. Fred could not do those things but they became great friends. They told each other their names. Fred was amazed when the other bird said his name was the thieving magpie. A few days later a man nearly shot Fred. He missed and shot a robin. The other two went mad and shot down to the man. Before he realized what was happening he was up in the air with one bird on each hand. They swooped down and let go of the man and SPLASH he landed in the duck pond and all the ducks were laughing at him. So he got out and tried to shoot them but the thieving magpie had taken the bullets out.'

2.22 As part of a class topic on an imaginary island an 8 year old boy wrote an account which well illustrates the sustained writing of which some older children in first schools are capable if given the opportunity:

'On the south and east sides of the island almost all the day you can hear the waves crashing on the rocks. Before the rollers hit the rocks I can see the white flecks of foam on the very top of them until they crash against the rocks and bounce off as spray. Behind the rocks there are granite rocks that at their highest they are a quarter of a mile high. On the east side of the island there are five caves. They are surrounded with rocks. Inside there are pools of stagnant water, also there are little trickles of water coming down to join the ever accumulating pools. The farther back into the cave you go the darker it gets. When you reach the back of the cave the water is deep enough to swim in. Along the north and west coasts there are the most beautiful sands that humans have ever set eyes upon. Only once have the pirates disturbed the peace of this beautiful place. During the day when the sun is at its hottest the sand sparkles as if it is millions of tiny granules of gold. Behind the sand there is a forest. On the sand there are shells of all descriptions. The shell that is the most common is the scallop and the sort of scallop is the queen scallop. But at the east end of the north coast the pirates have built a little quay and there is such a mess of old bottles, boots and goodness knows what else. I think it would be better to see the south coast than that.

Farther inland from the east side of the island there is a dense forest with parrots screeching, in the trees. I can see monkeys galore swinging from the tops of the trees. I can hear the crunching of the leaves underneath my feet. The wind is whistling through the trees, after the forest there are plains that spread as far as the eye can see. On one of the sides of the plain there is a dormant volcano. The next eruption will be in the year 2,000. On the other side of the plain there is a swamp. The swamp is so large that even a feather landing on it will sink. On the other side of the bog there is the pirates' camp. The strategy of the pirates is there is a coral reef round the island. The only opening is on the other side of the island and so the revenue men sail in through the gap and start searching, the pirates slip away using muffled oars. Beyond the volcano there is a waterfall so impressive that you have at least 20 pages of describing it but just let me say it is very impressive. The island is inhabited with 100 natives and 75 pirates.'

The development of writing

2.23 Teachers helped children in a variety of ways with their writing and, in a few cases, the difficult goal of giving real inspiration was achieved. Preliminary help was frequently given by providing an oral or visual stimulus and by discussion of the topic. While the writing was in progress most children received any necessary help to improve spelling and extend their vocabulary; at the same time the teachers gave a good deal of praise and encouragement. Effort and achievement were sometimes acknowledged by displaying samples of writing, or reading them to the class. On the other hand pupils sometimes worked in isolation, without the language stimulus that a skilful teacher can provide. Too often the introduction of new words seemed to be the main purpose of writing. Opportunities were seldom taken to introduce new syntactic structures to the children where, for example, a careful choice of topic or reading material might be used to introduce links of purpose, or cause and effect such as 'in order to', 'because', and 'so that'.

2.24 In some schools the children were producing a wide range of writing of quality, but in others there were examples of a lack of range and variety, of unproductive time being spent on English exercises, of a stifling of individuality by stereotyped tasks or copying, and of low levels of aspiration. Most schools at some time used English exercises from text books or commercially produced assignment cards. They were occasionally used with the youngest children but more commonly with the children of 7, 8 and 9. In some of the survey classes they were chosen with care and used in moderation but in many schools there was an excessive and purposeless use of this material. Often the exercises were little more than a means of occupying the children and it was rare to find them appropriate to the correction of individual errors made by the pupils in their personal writing. Where an emphasis was placed on formal exercises, as occurred in at least half of the schools, there was invariably too little opportunity for continuous writing.

2.25 Work cards made by teachers were used in many classes. Some of this material was carefully worded, appropriate to the children's age and ability and pleasant to use; some did not match the abilities of the children using it; some was visually unattractive. In some instances the children's work was seen to be stereotyped through the use of this type of material, particularly when the work card by its format gave children little or no opportunity to respond in an individual way, or in schools where heavy reliance was placed on work cards as the sole stimulus for a piece of writing.

2.26 The copying by young children of words and sentences written by their teachers is a necessary stage and is particularly appropriate when they are writing their own spoken words. However, copying from work books and cards occupied too great a part of the time of some 5 and 6 year olds. Older children spent even more time copying from cards or reading sheets, or from reference books, as part of individual projects. Sometimes passages encapsulating information given in a lesson were copied from the board. The copying kept the children busy and produced work of an apparently reasonable standard but it did not promote real progress in language development, or reveal what the children had remembered or understood.

Handwriting

2.27 In well over half of the 5 to 8 schools regular and suitable practice of handwriting was established by the time the children reached the age of seven or eight years; fewer of the 5 to 9 schools gave the necessary attention to the development of handwriting, and only a minority arranged for systematic and regular practice and teaching. There was little evidence that children were helped to produce an individual piece of handwriting that also had aesthetic and decorative value and in which they could take pride and from which they could gain satisfaction. Overall, with the younger age groups there was less consistency; some schools neglected steady practice of pattern and letter formation, and later work was adversely affected by this lack of groundwork. Even where a good allowance of time was given to routine practice, there was no certainty of high standards; both teaching and practice are important if a child's writing is to improve. 8 and 9 year old children might be expected by the end of their time in a first school to be writing a joined script; agreement with the middle school over questions of style is important. Children in the 5 to 8 schools seemed to achieve as effective a conversion to joined script as those in 5 to 9 schools.

Spelling

2.28 The majority of children achieved a good standard in spelling and help was given to all age groups through the teaching of phonics and spelling rules, the use of word lists, dictation, copying and the correction of errors. Occasional or more frequent testing of children from the age of 6 in spelling, often associated with learning lists or groups of words for homework, took place in over half of the 5 to

8 schools and in over three-quarters of the 5 to 9 schools. There was evidence that in these schools children were frequently going over ground already well-known or that they were being introduced to long lists of new words which were unlikely to be used in the context of current or planned work.

The use of audio-visual aids for language

2.29 At the time of the survey there was a good and plentiful supply of audio-visual equipment in most schools. Radio programmes were used extensively; television programmes were used less in the 5 to 8 schools than in the 5 to 9 schools.

2.30 Television was used as a support for reading in only a small number of schools. Where a television programme was used by more than one age range it often matched the level of ability of only a proportion of the viewing group; such programmes were often used as isolated experiences and there was seldom preparation or adequate follow up. Language teaching machines were occasionally used to give children additional help in consolidating early reading skills. Tape recorders were well used by children for listening to recorded stories and extracts from readers, or for recording original stories before these were made into reading books.

2.31 In some schools radio and television were used so much that children's complementary direct experiences were curtailed. When this was accompanied by under-preparation the children were gaining little for the time spent. A judicious use, however, produced some good work. In one school a story on radio, *A falling star,* was linked with a project on Red Indians and some interesting discussion took place.

Commentary

2.32 The teachers were concerned that children should learn to read and write; the standards achieved by many of the children were satisfactory. The supply of reading material was usually adequate and might include a range of reading materials made by the teachers, in addition to a good collection of attractive and suitable books. However, only a minority of children had ample time and opportunity to make full use of the books and to gain enjoyment from them. Young children were sometimes expected to practise the formal reading skills at too early an age, though there were examples of children who were fluent readers being helped to acquire more advanced reading skills. Extensive use of copy-writing, work cards and text books resulted in some children having too little time for personal writing. All children need frequent opportunities for writing of a descriptive and expressive kind.

2.33 Whatever a child's level of ability, the problem for the teacher is to provide a range of work that will call upon the child's existing skills and make a tolerable requirement for their extension. In reading and writing this calls for encouragement, enthusiasm and sensitive intervention on the part of the teacher. The use of a wider range of first hand experiences, both inside and outside the school is necessary if the children are to write progressively more fluently. In the teaching of reading it is important that there is a good readily accessible selection of books of quality which the children are encouraged to use freely.

LANGUAGE AND LITERACY — TALKING AND LISTENING

2.34 The importance of spoken language has already been referred to (2.3) and in all the classes the children were generally allowed to speak reasonably freely to each other, with their teachers and about their work with other adults and visitors; this was made possible by the informal atmosphere and the good personal relationships that existed. Although in general children were required to listen for a variety of purposes the demands made upon them varied considerably. Only a minority of schools consciously planned the work with the objective of promoting the improvement of listening skills. In classes where children too often engaged in individual assignments the practice not only reduced the kind of talking and listening which is engendered by shared experiences, but also curtailed the opportunities children had for listening to their teacher. On the other hand, the excessive noise which was tolerated in a few classes made it difficult for the teachers to talk to the children and for the children to listen or concentrate.

2.35 In the majority of schools the physical conditions for listening and talking were favourable but in a few inhibiting factors were noted. In some schools of open design too few enclosed spaces had been provided; in others children were restricted to working in the class bases without making use of shared facilities. Enclosed spaces such as conventional classrooms or discussion rooms in open plan buildings were advantageous to the development of listening skills.

2.36 Most children had the experience of listening in groups of different sizes, but a great deal of the listening took place within a class group. Listening as part of a large group naturally occurred in assembly in all the schools, but children were occasionally expected to listen for too long without responding and so became inattentive, and this also occurred in class lessons. Children of all ages, and especially young children, benefit from being given opportunities for discussion in small groups since it is easier for each to make a contribution and to feel an essential member of the group. More opportunities for small group discussion might usefully be arranged in the work of the schools.

2.37 Greater emphasis on class or larger group discussions might be expected as the children mature. In fact such discussions predominated for all age groups in the majority of classes. One of the main purposes of the discussions was to plan work and consider future activities. There were some fine examples of the sharing of first-hand experience, of recounting stories and of describing out of school activity. One 5 year old boy told the rest of the group about the similarities between his model, made of waste materials, and an oil rig that he had seen in Cornwall. In a class of 6 year olds, notions of symmetry were developed by the examination of examples, and by discussion of how an asymmetric object could be made symmetrical; the discussion was taken further by the introduction of a kaleidoscope. Some of the most searching oral work followed educational visits, talks from visitors such as the local policeman and radio or television programmes.

2.38 Visits to local places of interest such as museums and historic houses prompted spontaneous questions relating to the uses of antique implements, to the age of the buildings and to the people who originally lived in them. In preparation for these and other visits and with the help of sensitive prompting by a teacher, groups of children readily formulated their own questions.

2.39 In ten schools with substantial numbers of pupils from ethnic minority groups special help with English as a second language was given to those children who were non-English speaking or for whom English was their second language. In such schools, the arrangements for giving extra help to children from non-English speaking homes usually consisted of organising small withdrawal groups. In one school the help was given on a one-to-one basis. The quality of the work undertaken with these children was usually good. In isolated instances the additional staffing provided by the local education authority for ethnic minority children was used for other purposes such as additional reading practice for other children. In one school where a quarter of the children had serious problems with the English language because of their ethnic backgrounds, all the staff, including the welfare assistants, gave great attention throughout the day to helping the children to understand English and to use it effectively.

2.40 First schools are concerned to establish good links between home and school and to extend and build upon the language children have already acquired in the home. Where this language is not English this presents particular difficulties for the school, parents and children. These must not be underestimated. However, it was a matter of concern that in schools containing such pupils there was no evidence of constructive attempts to use the mother tongue to ease and make more effective the transition from home to school and from the language of the home into English.

2.41 Most teachers gave high priority to telling or reading stories to the children; stories were regarded as an essential part of the curriculum, and provided a source of real enjoyment for the large majority of children. Teachers generally used the opportunities created for the enrichment of language and the stimulus to the imagination to be gained from listening to a story. The younger children were dependent on the teacher providing stories for them to listen to but the older children also read their own. In the 5 to 8 schools most teachers arranged that children should have a daily story, though in a few schools this was not the case. In the 5 to 9 schools most children heard stories on a regular basis; the majority heard a story daily, but the frequency and regularity tended to decrease as the children grew older.

2.42 The children almost always heard stories as a class group, usually at the end of the afternoon session. Sometimes conditions and organisation were not conducive to the enjoyment of the story, for example when classes were put together and the group was too large. Occasionally classes of younger and older children were combined and in such cases the story that was read was often not suited to all the children because either the content, or the language, or both were too difficult or too simple for some.

2.43 Written guidelines on the choice of stories and how to use them were found in about half of the schools. In these schools the stories chosen usually contributed to a deepening of the children's understanding of people, the development of their imagination and an increased range of vicarious experience. In other schools there was no guidance on the choice of stories and how to use them; a haphazard selection often resulted in stories being used which lacked challenge, variety and quality. A small minority of the stories had little appeal for the children. The expectations of some schools contrasted markedly with those of others; some 7 year olds heard myths and legends and stories by good modern children's authors, while others were restricted to a diet of poorly written or retold tales. Very few schools introduced literature which reflected multi-cultural interests; where they did the stories were seldom related to any culture other than European. The stories used included Folk tales from other lands, Irish folk tales, and stories from Poland. The same stories were sometimes taken in the same way with different age groups in the same school; such repetition is unnecessary and restricts the children's range of experience.

Poetry

2.44 Although all the children listened frequently to stories, most had fewer opportunities to listen to poetry. Well chosen poetry can enrich language and develop the imagination, in addition to increasing children's sensitivity to people and their awareness of their surroundings. In the majority of schools poetry was not treated as an important aspect of the curriculum and most children heard it irregularly, and as an isolated experience.

2.45 Although in some classes the poetry sessions were well planned and anthologies were well chosen, in many classes the poems seemed to be picked at random. With the exception of the 5 years olds who often learned rhymes and jingles, few children were encouraged to learn poetry by heart. It was unusual for children to write poetry but in one school a collection of poems, including some good examples written by the children, was arranged under topics and was used by the staff to encourage other children to write.

2.46 In three-quarters of the classes of 5 year olds, children responded with enjoyment to nursery rhymes, action songs and counting rhymes. In exceptional cases the range was extended to include poems from good anthologies and by listening to tapes made from radio broadcasts. In slightly more than half of the 6 and 7 year old classes, poetry was read to the children; in a few classes there was a tendency to rely overmuch on comic verse. Poetry was introduced to three-quarters of the oldest children and there was a greater tendency for it to be related to other work, particularly topic work. Sometimes there were links with drama, for example 8 year old children acted out with enthusiasm *The king's breakfast*. Occasionally there were links with art, and sometimes children's writing was stimulated by the reading of poetry.

Drama and dramatic play

2.47 There was limited opportunity for the 5 and 6 year old children to engage in dramatic play. In almost half of the schools 'home corners' were inadequately equipped and unattractive and, almost inevitably, the quality of play was not good, though in a few classes it extended to include make-believe hospitals and shops as well as dressing-up clothes and building bricks. After a television programme on 'doctors', a 'surgery' was set up in one room and this led to lively discussions about doctors. The children talked freely about their experiences and illnesses and such things as thermometers and stethoscopes were explained. However, in general, there was little evidence of the development of imaginative and dramatic play; teachers rarely intervened or took part, and it was not unusual for teachers to be engaged in other activities, such as hearing children read, while such play was taking place.

2.48 Dressing-up boxes were found in a number of class-rooms; they varied considerably in the range and quality of the materials provided and in the use that was made of them. Sometimes schools possessed a large number of costumes of quality which stimulated work of a high standard. In one instance these were kept in a central position in the school and used for school plays, seasonal productions, school assemblies and for class drama.

2.49 The dramatisation of nursery rhymes, action songs and traditional stories occurred in many of the classes for the youngest children. The dramatisation of stories took place with all age groups but seldom on a regular basis. Sometimes this work included mime, sometimes spontaneous exchanges or words suggested by the teacher. Biblical stories and topics related to religious education were dramatised by children of all ages and it was fairly common for plays of this kind to be part of an assembly taken by an individual class. Stories linked with history, famous people and literature were interpreted through drama by a few of the older children.

2.50 Nativity plays were presented to parents in most schools; apart from this, school dramatic or musical productions featured in a minority of schools and usually involved the oldest children and a group of staff. Occasionally drama provided a valuable link with other parts of the curriculum and resulted in language, movement, art and crafts and music contributing to the dramatic production. In one school the 9 year olds visited a seventeenth century mansion and dressed up to play the role of children of that period. Some children received visits from drama groups or visited local theatres to see live performances or to watch puppet shows; performances of this kind provided a valuable stimulus for language development.

2.52 Puppets were made in very few classes; sometimes the children created a character and adopted its role in a simple play; sometimes the puppets remained unused.

Commentary

2.53 Speaking and listening, essential activities in all schools, are most successful when made to contribute to children's understanding. Those children able to find the best words and put them in the best order to express their feelings and their ideas had been introduced by their teachers to a carefully planned range of experiences valuable in themselves and requiring children to extend their powers of language.

2.54 While it is unlikely that every opportunity for extending language will be taken by teachers or children, in the liveliest schools oral language development occurs every day and throughout the curriculum.

MATHEMATICS

The attention given to mathematical skills and concepts

2.55 In the schools generally, and with all age groups, emphasis was put on work relating to number patterns and relationships, calculations in the four rules, measurement, and working with money and with shapes. The range of work in the mathematics curriculum widened for the children as they grew older.

2.56 Nearly all children of every age and ability achieved a satisfactory standard in the practice of computation. The youngest children spent a considerable amount of time learning to count, to recognise simple number patterns and number symbols, to use a number line and to understand the elements of place value. Practical activities involving sorting and classifying, ordering and matching were introduced in the majority of classes. This work was continued and extended with the 6 and 7 year olds to include numbers up to *20*, more advanced work with number patterns, and the use of number squares. Counting forwards and backwards, counting in *2s, 3s, 4s, 5s,* and *6s,* and work on odds, evens, pairs and doubling numbers also occurred. The work of the 8 and 9 year olds included working with numbers up to *100*, work with multiples, divisors and factors and work in different number bases; the 9 year olds frequently used larger numbers in more complex calculations.

2.57 Practical activities requiring the use of the four rules to be found in the work for some children of all age levels, though the peak period of the introduction of these activities was for 6 to 8 year olds in the 5 to 8 schools, but only the 6 and 7 year olds in the 5 to 9 schools. Those 5 year olds given access to practical activities made tallies, demonstrated 'more than' and 'less than' and made simple pictorial and block graphs. The practical activities, where they existed, of the 6 and 7 year olds involved the use of a simple abacus and of other apparatus for work in addition and subtraction; those of the 8 and 9 year olds included temperature recordings and curve stitching and were associated with work using the four rules.

2.58 The schools aimed to develop a thorough knowledge of number bonds from *0-20,* and almost all children, from an early age, performed calculations accurately. The work of the youngest children included the addition and subtraction of numbers up to *10,* sometimes resulting in answers up to *20.* At the age of 6 some children were adding and subtracting with "carrying" between columns, multiplying numbers up to *20,* and dividing by sharing and grouping. At the age of 7 further calculation in the four rules was successfully undertaken, with some children working in hundreds, tens and units with a carrying figure in addition and subtraction. The tables of multiplication by *2* and *3* were often learned by heart. With 8 and 9 year olds computation in the four rules was extended and there was work on place value in three-digit numbers. Work with the tables of *2, 3, 4, 5* and *10* was included and the more able children were undertaking multiplication and division by the other numbers up to *12.* Work involving two places of decimals, as in pounds and pence, was included in the work of the oldest children, particularly the 9 year olds.

2.59 The work on fractions occurred mainly in the oldest classes in the schools. If practical work with the youngest children had included such activities as cooking these might have more often given rise to discussion of halves and quarters. Some 7 year olds were introduced to halves, quarters and thirds through colouring shapes in work books or more effectively through a practical activity. The more able 8 and 9 year olds successfully worked with fifths, sixths, eighths, tenths and sixteenths, though this was not always associated with practical work.

2.60 Appropriate work in the measurement of length and time and, to a lesser extent, of weight and capacity was undertaken by all age groups in the majority of schools and often included practical work and activities directly relating to the children's current interests and topics. Measuring by the youngest children was often in non-standard measures such as handspans, strides and lengths of their own feet. Those involved measured rooms and objects within the school or their own height, and through these activities they acquired a more precise understanding of words like 'long', 'short', 'large', 'small', 'tall', 'wide', 'narrow'. The 6 and 7 year olds were usually introduced to standard measures such as the metre and centimetre, and used metre sticks and trundle wheels for measuring longer distances.

2.61 Through handling a variety of objects and the use of balances and scales the young children were helped to develop concepts of 'heavy' and 'light'. Non-standard units were replaced by standard weights for the older children when weighing parcels and comparing their weights, or weighing disparate objects.

2.62 Play with water and a variety of containers was particularly important in giving the 5 year olds an early appreciation of capacity. This work was developed for the older children by the introduction of imperial or metric measures.

2.63 Children usually learned to tell the time first by work on hours and half hours, followed by work on quarter hours, and then minutes to and past the hour. Many older children worked on timetables and calendars.

2.64 To learn calculations involving money, 5 year olds engaged in shopping activities, sometimes in the class shop and were able to carry out simple purchases mainly with coins up to 10p. Shopping problems for 6 and 7 year olds called for the practical use of money up to £1, the purchase of a specified number of items and giving change. Some of the 6 and 7 year olds, as well as the 8 and 9 year olds were proficient in written money calculations, written shopping problems and simple calculations in the four rules.

2.65 Where work on two- and three-dimensional shapes, spatial relationships and symmetry was undertaken 5 and 6 year olds sorted and matched shapes, made patterns with shapes, did simple work on symmetry and learned to recognise simple two- or three-dimensional shapes such as triangles, squares, circles, rectangles, cubes and cylinders. 7 year olds made patterns with regular shapes, and studied the more obvious properties of a variety of shapes. With the 8 year olds this occasionally included terms such as 'vertices', an introduction to the idea of area, including tessellation, and to obtuse and acute angles.

2.66 It was unusual to find the children first estimating an answer then calculating and later comparing the results. This procedure was used by the oldest children in some 5 to 9 schools but little was done in the 5 to 8 schools. From the age of 7 the children in a few classes were estimating accurately length, weight, capacity and time before embarking on measurement.

2.67 In a quarter of the schools the children had covered a considerable range of work in mathematics by the time they reached the end of their time at the first school. Many other schools were concentrating on computation to such an extent that children lacked opportunities to apply mathematical ideas to everyday experiences and sometimes failed to understand the calculations they undertook.

The balance between the acquisition and use of computational skills

2.68 In a fifth of the schools there was, throughout, a good balance between learning how to perform a calculation and using it in a practical setting, either within mathematics or elsewhere in the curriculum. In the remaining four-fifths a good balance was not achieved, and skills were practised in isolation; the work was usually based on self-contained commercially produced schemes or on graded work cards made in the school. Computation often formed the main element in the work; in some schools the sole aim was for the children to reach a standard of efficiency in abstract calculations, though even in these an element of practical work was occasionally included. There was also evidence that children were required to use abstract ideas without the practical experience necessary to a working understanding of them. Younger children were as likely to practise mathematical skills in isolation as were the older children.

Children's play and the use of incidental interest for mathematical learning

2.69 In six schools the mathematics in all the classes was related to the children's interests and experiences and the teachers were making very positive efforts to introduce mathematical ideas in an interesting way and in relation to everyday things. In nearly half the schools such practice was found in some classes. Whether the opportunities were recognised and used to develop the children's understanding of mathematics depended less on the school's policy and planning than on the perception and expertise of the individual teacher.

2.70 The domestic play of the young children seen in some of the schools provided many opportunities for developing mathematical concepts. Laying the table, the sorting of equipment, and the matching of the clothes to the size of the dolls were used to help establish the idea of one-to-one correspondence and ordering by size. The baking of bread provided opportunities for measuring the time it took the yeast to rise, dividing the dough into tins, estimating the size of the loaf in relation to the amount of dough in the baking tin, and timing and baking. A group of children growing strawberries estimated the number of strawberries the plant might produce, whether they would 'go round the class', and used paper circles to represent strawberries to determine how many would be required. In the end one child said "We shall have to buy some". In other schools use of materials such as sand, water, building bricks and other constructional materials provided the opportunity for introducing words relating to numbers, size, shape and capacity. The making of models required the selection of boxes of the right size and shape; the painting of life size figures led children to measure their limbs, head and trunk. The making and stocking of toy shops, pet shops and grocers' shops stimulated work on size, shape and measurement, in addition to work with money. Routine counting tasks, (for example, counting the number of milk bottles each day and checking returned items of equipment such as scissors) turned these chores into useful mathematical practice for the children.

2.71 One group of 7 year olds used a stop watch for the counting and timing of skipping; model cars made by another group were raced and the results plotted on graph paper. As part of a project on air, balloons were used in an experiment to calculate time and distance. Groups of 8 year olds became interested in the formations in square dancing; in the foreign money brought in by several children whose fathers were seamen; and in the positioning of television cameras for the best angle for photography after a visit to an international football match at Wembley.

2.72 Only just over half the schools made any links between mathematics and other areas of the curriculum. These links were more often found in the work of the older children whose wider interests supported work on general topics and provided opportunities for developing a variety of mathematical ideas.

2.73 What can be done was shown by one school where much of the work in science with the older pupils was recorded on graphs or charts: for example as part of a project on teeth, a graph depicted the number of fillings each child had. In another, work on an imaginary island called for the use of coordinates to locate the position of geographical features, and work in art on reflections was done alongside mathematical work on symmetry. 8 year old children derived some idea of scale by studying a 6-inch ordnance survey map alongside an aerial photograph of the locality. One class measured the heights of the village church and the community hall and studied the use of triangular shapes in the beam supports; another class studied the relevance of certain shapes in everyday use, for example in boxes and buildings. Visits provided further opportunities; one to the seaside for 9 year olds involved, for example, a calculation of distance and speed of travelling.

2.74 The mathematical work of the 5 and 6 year old children included links with physical education and movement, such as counting steps and jumps and making shapes with their bodies. After a television programme on David and Goliath the children measured out Goliath's height and discussed the current standard measures. A class collected flowers in a local orchard and the children grouped them according to the species, counted them and commented upon their size. As part of a topic on the Vikings 7 year old children marked out a Viking ship to scale in the playground. Three able 7 year olds in one class made a scale plan of the school. A group of the same age undertook a study of trees and wood which included the measurement of leaf size and area, the weight of a log, and counting ring growth. In other classes a topic on 'Shopping' was introduced with a visit to the local shops where the children used money; block graphs depicted progress in swimming; and work with 9 year olds included more detailed weather recording and the use of maximum and minimum thermometers. Work in history gave rise to the need for symbolic representation of varying lengths of historical periods; development in science and art included controlled experiments with the germination of seeds, and patterns of shape and symmetry in drawing from nature.

2.75 In schools and classes where play was undervalued the mathematical possibilities of children's play were not developed. Where children's interests and activities, including those stimulated by work on specific topics, did not include mathematics elements, mathematics was usually regarded as separate from the children's everyday experiences, or there was an over-emphasis on formal mathematics and an over-reliance on work cards, or an adherence to an assignment system. Many teachers did not sufficiently encourage individual, independent investigations; this suggested a lack of confidence in extending the investigations or utilising the discoveries and it should continue to be an objective of in-service training to increase the teacher's confidence.

Visual aids and displays

2.76 Displays provided by teachers or occasionally constructed by the children made a valuable contribution in the teaching of mathematics for all age groups and were used in more than three-quarters of the classes. The most common forms of display for the 5, 6 and 7 year olds were the number line and the frieze, and for the older children graphical representation and number squares. With the younger age groups a number of the displays reflected the individual interests of the children, with charts recording such things as personal and family characteristics, or the children's activities, or discoveries relating to time, capacity, money and spatial awareness. The concepts of size and shape were furthered by the collections of two- and three-dimensional objects and by charts of large and small objects, as well as by models made from waste materials and by constructional toys. Number charts and friezes were sometimes linked with work in English, as for instance a frieze depicting the rhyme 'As I was going to St Ives I met a man with seven wives'. The displays in the 7 year old classes indicated an extension of work on topics such as symmetry, spirals, tessellations, wheels and maps. In the classes of older children the displays reflected their widening interests and developing skills, and included material on a specific historical period and the dating of local houses, the metric packaging of goods, the making of magnetic needles, and the use of maps and tables giving the time of the tides as part of a project based on the sea shore.

Continuity of work

2.77 In approximately half of the schools considerable thought had been given to planning the work and its progression with the result that there was adequate continuity of work in mathematics. This was often supported by the use of guidelines and by staff discussions. The teachers' knowledge of individual children, and a willingness to diverge from the basic scheme to meet the needs of individuals or groups, helped children proceed with understanding and confidence. This was reinforced by the use of carefully graded daily assignments, of appropriate equipment and of school-produced work cards. Checklists and the recording of children's progress helped to ensure that the work was matched to the ability and pace of work of individual children. The proper use of commercially produced mathematics schemes and text books was the basis of continuity in the work in some schools.

2.78 Occasionally continuity was sought only in specific areas of work, usually number and computation. Failures in progression were most common when there were no guidelines or schemes. Inadequate attention to continuity usually led to insufficient uniformity in methods and the haphazard setting of tasks, resulting in retrograde steps and unnecessary repetition. There was more likelihood of this occurring where planning was based only on the informal transmission of information between teachers or was dependent on teachers' memories.

Resources

2.79 At the time of the survey the provision of mathematics equipment and materials was good or adequate in all the classes in 65 schools. In five schools the provision was adequate in some of the classes; in these schools it could be either the older or the younger children who suffered from lack of equipment. Nearly one in eight of the schools was poorly equipped for mathematics in all classes. In schools where the provision was good there was a wide and varied selection of materials and apparatus readily available for all age groups, often well stored and clearly labelled. In most schools each class had its own apparatus and materials for counting, weighing, measuring and for work on time, capacity, money and shape. In a few schools a resource area shared by two or more classes contained material that could be borrowed by individual classes. There were a few instances of mathematics rooms which had been created from spare classrooms and equipped with a generous supply of materials and apparatus. The resource areas usually contained a wider range of equipment than could be provided in one class but lack of careful planning sometimes meant that the equipment was underused.

2.80 In a quarter of the schools the mathematics equipment was used well and effectively; in such schools the practical work was part of the planned policy of the school and was required by the scheme of work. The teachers recognised its value, sufficient time and opportunity were given for the children to use the equipment and adequate help was given to them in both its selection and use. However, in more than half the schools a bias towards written practice of computation and a concentration on other aspects of the curriculum left little time for the use of equipment; or its effective use in practical work was undermined by the lack of guidance given to the children.

Commentary

2.81 By about age 8 or 9 children were generally familiar with numbers up to *100* and able to compute accurately. Some work was done in fractions which might, in simple and practical ways, have begun earlier; more might also have been attempted on shape.

2.82 Children of all ages spent too little time applying numerical skills, and too little was made of the mathematical opportunities in children's play and in topic work. By the age of 8 or 9 the children in about a quarter of the schools had effectively covered a considerable range of work, but in only a fifth of the schools was there a good balance between the practice and application of skills.

2.83 Planned progression and continuity were evident in mathematics in only half of the schools in the survey. In mathematics, as in other areas of the curriculum, careful planning, the use of effective guidelines and record keeping can do much to help the children's progress at an appropriate pace with understanding and confidence.

RELIGIOUS AND MORAL EDUCATION

Assembly

2.84 Assemblies were held in all the schools and in most of them were regarded by the staff as important occasions; often they provided the focal point for all the religious education in the school and in some instances they provided the only tangible evidence that such work was undertaken. However, there was great variety in the timing and duration of assemblies and attendance at them. Children in many schools came together at the beginning of the school day. On social and educational grounds some heads had decided that young children gained from starting the day within their class groups, and therefore assemblies were held at the end of the morning or in the afternoon.

2.85 The leadership of the assembly was frequently undertaken by heads but in a number of schools, senior staff or members of the clergy had an important role. In many schools assembly took the form of an act of worship. In others it was less overtly religious in character, but in both cases there was a strong sense of assembly as a community gathering in which children and teachers, and often parents too, shared. Assemblies usually included well chosen hymns, prayers — sometimes written by children — a story, poems or a talk. Children's birthdays were celebrated, music and drama were introduced, and the occasion was often used to enable children to relate the experiences of individual classes, show pictures, models or items from an interest table or read their own stories.

2.86 Many of the assemblies were based on themes from the Bible or on moral values relevant to the children's lives both within and outside the school community. Appreciation of the seasons, the natural world and the care of living things were topics frequently used in assemblies and for which collections of flowers and fruits, pictures and animals provided the visual focus. One assembly based on 'Why I like life' was taken by 8 year olds who read to the school their lively and individual writing reflecting the range of their interests. The practice of children leading assemblies was common to most schools; and these assemblies were often carefully prepared and enjoyable occasions, sometimes enhanced by the presence of parents.

2.87 Music was generally included in assembly; recorded music was played when the children were entering or leaving the hall and the children sang to the accompaniment of the piano; additionally in 48 schools, groups of children played recorders, guitars or percussion instruments. In nearly all the schools the children's singing in assembly was lively and tuneful especially when modern hymn tunes were used. In a few instances the appreciation of music was a particularly important feature, as for example when a table was set up in the hall giving information about Mozart — the composer for the week — the title of the day's music, and writing and pictures by the children about him and the instruments. The assembly began with part of a recording of one of his horn concertos.

2.88 In 39 of the schools there were pupils from ethnic minority groups, mainly Asian, West Indian and African. In some of these schools where the number of children of different faiths was small their presence was not taken into account in assembly. Even in the small group of schools where quite a high proportion of children were members of ethnic minorities, relatively little had been done to acknowledge religious and cultural differences or to become familiar with the background of the pupils. In isolated instances there was a recognition of Muslim and Sikh festivals. There was in general little awareness in schools of the changing nature of the community or any recognition of the diversity of cultures and faiths represented.

The teaching of religious education

2.89 Approximately half the schools specified time for work in religious education but often there was little evidence to suggest that the work was being done. In some schools which did set aside time for this subject the amount differed from one age group to another; a few classes had regular times for religious education while other classes in the same school had no set periods.

2.90 Of the schools which did not provide a set place in the programme for religious education, except for assemblies, some ensured that work in this area of the curriculum was undertaken at least once each week. In these schools the work was not necessarily done at the same time each week; other schools preferred to approach religious education "incidentally, as opportunities arose". Many heads and teachers had moved towards implicit forms of religious education, woven into the whole curriculum and life of the school and the relationships within it. However, the lack of timetabling made it uncertain whether the necessary teaching was being included. The traditional approach took popular Bible stories, often in a random order, and used them in assemblies and with individual classes; these were supplemented by stories associated with the main Christian festivals. Literature other than the Bible played only a small part in religious education in most schools though there were, exceptionally, examples of myths, legends and stories of the saints being used. In only a small proportion of the schools were resources for religious education of good quality and range.

2.91 There was little evidence of the development of appropriate thematic work in religious education apart from a few examples of topics such as the seasons, living things, the senses, homes and families. The work on these topics sometimes stemmed from suggestions in recently revised agreed syllabuses. Other religious and moral education was based on themes such as 'Helping the sick and the elderly' used in the assemblies. Work of this nature was sometimes followed up in a practical way by inviting elderly people to concerts and assemblies. Occasionally discussions were held on helping people in need in many parts of the world. In some classes specific religious education appeared to occur only when teachers were helping children to prepare class assemblies.

Personal awareness and growth

2.92 In almost every school there was evidence of good social relationships. In most schools some children were being helped to develop self-confidence, independence, and an awareness of their strengths and weaknesses in ways that also encouraged a better understanding of others and a concern for them — though unfortunately this did not often include an appreciation of the beliefs and traditions of people of other ethnic backgrounds.

2.93 Most of the schools gave the children some contributory role in the school community, at least on routine monitorial duties such as milk distribution, tidying up, giving out materials. In a minority of schools the children were encouraged to take some responsibility for choosing an activity or pursuing a programme or work. It was unusual for the responsibility to be related to the children's maturity although occasionally older children helped the younger, notably at meal times. There was no general agreement about when children were likely to be ready for certain kinds of responsibility, to become self-reliant, or to take responsibility for their own behaviour and work without close supervision. Some teachers expected this kind of behaviour from most 5 year olds and were not disappointed, others found it beyond 9 year olds. Children's capabilities were more likely to be under- than over-estimated.

Commentary

2.94 Every school in the survey was concerned to promote good relationships between the children and teachers, and almost all succeeded. An awareness of moral values was encouraged, and in many instances this was made explicit with the help of well-planned assemblies.

2.95 Many schools in the survey used assembly as the main vehicle for religious education in the school and had little classroom work in the subject. There were some children from ethnic minority groups in about half the schools in the survey; their presence was rarely taken into account in religious education. It is important that all children should be helped to develop an understanding and awareness of the cultures and faiths represented in the community.

LEARNING ABOUT PEOPLE

Themselves

2.96 With all age groups a number of topics furthered the children's understanding of themselves and their bodies and included work on the senses. A class of 9 year olds experimented with a variety of tastes using sugar, salt, lemon and vinegar and this led to an examination of the sensitive structure of the tongue. Sight was also studied and involved the children working in pairs and doing simple experiments such as noting the changes in the size of their pupils immediately after opening their eyes.

2.97 Although health education was more likely to be timetabled for the older than the younger children, incidental work on diet, teeth and hand washing occurred with all age groups. Physical education lessons prompted consideration of such things as breathing, posture, and pulse rates. Health, nutrition, teeth and eyes were amongst topics studied by classes of older children. Careful preparation for the visits of the doctor and the dentist was undertaken in some schools. The Schools Council Project 'All about me' and radio and television programmes were used as part of the health education programme in a minority of schools.

Others

2.98 Teachers introduced children, in various degrees, to the different contributions individuals make to the local and wider community; to the effect of environmental conditions on the ways in which people live; and to changes that have occurred in the course of time. It would be pretentious to label work of this kind, done with 5 or 6 year olds, as social studies, geography or history, but some of the skills, ideas and knowledge associated with these subjects were in some of the work, and by the time pupils were 8 or 9, were more apparent. That they were not always easy to disentangle is evident in the following descriptions.

The locality

2.99 Opportunities were given to children throughout the age range to enquire about the ways in which the local environment affected the peoples' lives and influenced occupations. An interest in the work of local people such as the postman, fireman, farmer and doctor was sometimes extended by a visit from one of these people or by a visit to their place of work. Where children were able to use first-hand experience of a place and make their own observations and collections of material, and were given information and explanations from people they met, the work gained in meaning and became evidently more satisfying for the children.

2.100 A group of 7 year olds was helped to understand better the nature of the local community when, as part of a project, they made pictorial maps of their journey from home to school with drawings of the important buildings passed. From the age of 7 many of the children undertaking a study of their area were introduced to local maps. Some children made models of their houses and other buildings, noted their functions, and stuck them on to a map. In one school an excellent aerial photograph of the school and its surrounding area was used by children to locate the different parts of the school, their homes and local shops. One class who visited a nearby church gained an aerial view when they looked down on the area from the top of the tower.

More distant places

2.101 Holidays, holiday postcards and journeys undertaken aroused considerable interest in all age groups and maps were sometimes used to indicate routes and resorts. Topics being studied by some children reflected current events and were often linked to a study of the lives of people in other lands. As a result of the Queen's visit to the Middle East a class of 9 year olds were studying Bedouin Arabs. The children made a frieze and a collection of interesting news items and photographs of Arab life. The International Year of the Child also provided the stimulus for an interest in children from other countries and led to work with world maps and national flags. Work on Germany in a 7 year old class included mounting a display of products, learning simple German words, children's stories and traditions, hearing personal recollections by the children and viewing a film shown by a parent. After seeing a television programme a class of 9 year olds studied a map of Palestine and estimated and compared distances such as the length and breadth of the Sea of Galilee and the distances between towns associated with the life of Jesus. Maps of Europe and of the world were used in other classes and the children produced their own notebooks within which they included duplicated maps.

People in other times

2.102 In one class of 7 year olds a discussion about 'Life in olden times' had begun with the children talking about themselves and their earliest memories and then about their parents' recollections of childhood. Artefacts were collected and labelled. The discussion introduced the names of kings and queens of the past and used a chart of Queen Victoria's family relationships. The opportunity was taken to introduce Roman numerals, as in George V.

2.103 Local residents were enlisted to bring the past alive for some children. Grandparents were often willing to help in this way; one told a class of 8 year olds about the second world war, and another grandfather recalled his childhood experiences for a class of 6 year olds. After a visit to the school by the local police a class of 8 year olds developed an interest in Robert Peel, and in the origin and history of the police force.

2.104 In ten schools collections of articles from the past such as clothes and coins stimulated discussion. Wall displays or artefacts that the children could examine helped them to understand the domestic life and the work of people who lived in previous eras. One 8 year old class made a collection including a miner's helmet and lamp, a flat iron, a griddle and an old Bible all used by local people in times past. The population explosion in 1830-40 and the development of the railways were referred to in the study. After seeing a television programme on the Victorians, 7 and 8 year olds collected period clocks, clothing, kitchen utensils and old photographs; they made fabric pictures and models out of waste materials of various forms of transport; they used reference books and visited museums. Following the same programme a class of 9 year olds learned some Victorian songs; a good collection of books was used together with items supplied by a local museum to support the work.

2.105 The children's understanding of the way people used to live was also increased through visits, especially when there was adequate preparation and follow-up. Some classes went to local museums, castles and churches. Such work often included making simple written and pictorial records. One group of older children made drawings of carriages after a visit to a local estate. Environmental studies in a number of 8 and 9 year old classes helped to link historical and geographical ideas and provided the opportunity to use old maps and study old buildings. One study included visits to the village church and chapel, during which local people talked to the children about the buildings and the contents. The former school building was visited and elderly village residents described their experiences in the 'old' school. The children wrote factual accounts of what they had seen and heard, using information given by local people, extracts from a pamphlet written about the church, brass rubbings, drawings and models.

2.106 Visits to historic houses and local industries were undertaken by older children. One of the interestings visits enjoyed by the 8 and 9 year olds was to a seventeenth century mansion where the children dressed in the clothes of the period and lived for one day as the children of that period would have lived. A class of 9 year olds followed a visit to an industrial museum with a study of the development of mechanised transport.

2.107 In isolated cases, legends, folk stories and Bible stories were used to develop an understanding of the past. The work for some children included stories of famous people. Work on the topic "King Arthur" involved 8 year olds in making a large pictorial map of Camelot showing the river, road, castle and travellers.

Commentary

2.108 The examples of work described in the preceding paragraphs took place during the course of the survey or figured in the children's written work in the months immediately before it. Few were unique, in kind at any rate, to a single school, though no school would want to or could undertake them all. They show what children in first schools could be interested in, and can do given imaginative, knowledgeable and energetic teaching. Too many schools do too little to draw children's attention to the wider circumstances in which they live or to the past, or they too often use radio and television programmes for which the children are insufficiently prepared, and following which they do little but recount what they have heard or seen.

2.109 In schools where children were learning effectively about people the most successful topics were those in which the children were given a sense of immediacy, that included work on their home areas, that introduced the experiences of local people and included artefacts that could be compared with those in current use. In this way the concept of change was introduced, and the children were helped to appreciate similarities and differences in human behaviour.

2.110 There were few 5 and 6 year old classes where the children were learning much about the past. In view of the difficulty experienced by young children in appreciating time scale or in acquiring a sense of chronological order this was understandable. However, there was, in general, a lack of appreciation of suitable work that could be done with the younger children using, for example, recollections of parents and grandparents. In nearly half of the 7 year old classes children were given opportunities to learn about the past. Topics arising from television programmes, local visits or current events formed the subject of work in approximately a quarter of the 7 year old classes. Work that could be identified specifically as relating to the past increased further with the older age groups and work of a historical nature was included in three-quarters of the 8 year old classes and in nearly all of the 9 year old classes. History was more likely to be timetabled for the 8 and 9 year olds.

2.111 Even the older children were seldom being helped towards an appreciation of chronological order. Some were introduced to different periods of history through work on cavemen, the Stone Age, the Vikings and the Romans without being made aware of their relative positions on the historical time scale. Other children started with a study of the Victorians and worked backwards in time. Too much of the work on topics selected by individual teachers or suggested by television programmes was not part of a coordinated school plan and tended to be fragmented and superficial.

LEARNING ABOUT THE PHYSICAL WORLD

2.112 A considerable amount of school time, much more in some schools than in others, was given to learning about the physical and natural environment through direct experience, through being told and through reading; what was learned was talked over, written about, illustrated and modelled.

2.113 Practical work associated with mathematics was important in helping children to distinguish and classify things around them by shape, size, weight and temperature, and a variety of activities led children to be aware that common materials have different characteristics and may be suited to different uses. In the relatively few schools where it occurred, direct observation of plants and animals, for the purposes of painting and modelling them, drew children's attention to previously unnoticed details of shape, colour and texture. Tending school pets and gardens brought to light the basic needs of living things. Simple studies of the school, its grounds and neighbourhood increased children's awareness of the nature of the local landscape and climate; visits further afield, when well used, added to their knowledge.

2.114 The following section of the report concentrates on examples concerned with learning about the landscape and weather and represents early stages of the study of physical geography, and learning about the behaviour of materials, animals and plants, and incorporates the beginnings of science.

2.115 Work that could be identified as dealing with embryonic geographical concepts and skills occurred in more than half of the 5 and 6 year old classes, in a greater number of the 7 year old classes, and in nearly all of the classes for 8 and 9 year olds. The very elementary work of the 5 year olds was gradually made more systematic as children went through school.

Plans, maps, globes and models

2.116 Most schools included in their programme activities which might focus children's attention on space and distance — within the school buildings, in the playground and on walks in the locality; mathematical experiences further increased their understanding of spatial concepts.

2.117 There was, however, a lack of appreciation of the range of appropriate work that could have been provided for younger children. Although many of them had access to models and plans of farms, roads, railways, runways and docks and they used bricks, sand and construction sets, such resources were seldom used to represent the local area, or to interpret pictures in information books, or to relate to experience gained on visits. These resources were often used for imaginative play, but, as a result of the lack of appropriate intervention by the teacher, the potential for developing spatial concepts, especially those leading to the idea of scale, was seldom realised.

2.118 Children were often introduced to the making of plans and maps by drawing plans of the classroom and school. The next stage in map-making is not easy but there were examples of careful preparation. Some were referred to earlier (paragraph 2.100). Visits to places of interest such as zoos, churches, museums, castles and holiday resorts often stimulated the production or use of simple road maps of the kind motorists use. In many classes for 9 year olds, and in fewer of the 8 year olds, globes and maps, including ordnance survey maps, were available, but these were not always used. The work with maps was seldom concerned with contours, though examples did occur.

2.119 One representation was made by a class of 9 year olds during their study of the nearby sea-shore. They made a transect of the beach, and kept records of the tides. This piece of work was planned with clearly identified skills, knowledge and ideas to be acquired and stages of work were set out in advance; this no doubt contributed to the success of the project.

The weather

2.120 Children are interested in the weather from an early age and many of the youngest children noted and recorded general weather conditions each day. More detailed and precise observations and written records were made by the older children. Air temperatures became an absorbing interest with many children,particularly in view of the low temperatures during the winter months of the survey. Prolonged periods of snow, ice and frost created problems for living and hazards for travelling, which were used by many teachers to increase the children's understanding of weather conditions. In most schools children used thermometers to record temperature and a number of them brought snow and ice into the classrooms and recorded the time required for melting them in different conditions. A class of 6 year olds worked on a topic on 'Winter Clothes', 7 year olds studied snow footprints and many older children became interested in icebergs. Summer temperatures and hours of sunshine were also of general interest and work on shadows, often requiring careful measurement, was undertaken by children of various ages. Older children in some schools were interested in cloud formation; a few were able to read weather maps. The work of a few of the older children included accurate observations and recordings based on their own use of such equipment as maximum and minimum thermometers, sun dials, magnetic compasses, rain gauges and anemometers. The skills they required for these activities showed an appropriate advance on the simple weather chart of the 5 year old children.

LEARNING ABOUT MATERIALS, PLANTS AND ANIMALS

2.121 Natural specimens and objects brought into school by children and radio and television broadcasts were the usual means of introducing scientific interests. When children noticed things for the first time about materials, plants or animals, they were often encouraged to described their findings and good discussions usually followed, as when a class of 5 year old children observed the insects that had fallen out of a shaken tree. Frequently, however, incidental opportunities to develop a scientific approach and experiment were not used and only a minority of schools operated a planned course. Children were rarely encouraged to think about their observations by looking for patterns or by making predictions which they might then test. With the older children promising work was too often left undeveloped and the scientific potential was not exploited.

2.122 Most schools had at least a small quantity of simple, useful science equipment, and in about a quarter of the schools the quantity and quality were adequate or good. The most common stock included magnets, magnifiers, mirrors, thermometers and simple electrical equipment such as switches, batteries and bulbs. Materials such as sand, water, building bricks and pulleys which lend themselves to scientific experiment and the development of scientific thinking were available in many classes for the younger age groups. Sand and water were less often available to children over the age of 5, and so it was unusual for the older children to meet scientific ideas during incidental play. Schools did not always make full use of their resources when either basic equipment or expensive items or both were stored centrally. In these instances the equipment was not always easily accessible to the youngest children.

Heat and energy

2.123 Any work on heat needs especially careful supervision, of the kind that was seen in a class of 7 to 9 year olds. In this class an effect of heat as warm air rising from a candle turned a suspended circular fan was observed. The work also showed the importance of oxygen to burning and drew attention to the different extents to which various materials retained heat. The results of the work were shown graphically.

2.124 Work was undertaken by 8 and 9 year olds who kept bread and milk at different temperatures for four days and noted the changes in the colour, size and smell of the moulds. This led to discussions on micro-organisms and the making of yoghurt. Some work was based on reference books and could be sustained over a considerable period of time, as for example, that of a class of 8 and 9 year olds based on a project on 'Energy' which dealt with coal, oil and nuclear fuels. It included descriptive writing, drawing and painting and gathering information from books.

The use and operation of machines

2.125 Only a few examples were seen of work on the use and operation of machines. A class of 7 year olds studying wheels, cycles and machines made models, including some that worked, from waste materials, drew pictures and made written records. They talked about machines used in the home and read from a specially arranged book collection, which included books on great inventions and on mechanics; in doing so they added to their vocabulary and to their ability to describe.

2.126 After watching a television programme some children made models of a helicopter and a biplane. Other children made working models out of constructional materials; these could be used more often than they are to develop ideas, for example, of leverage and to observe the characteristics of the material used.

Water

2.127 Water has a particular fascination for young children and its use occasionally led to work of a scientific kind. Some 9 year olds became interested in filtering muddy water to make it less impure. Two boys of the same age had an extensive knowledge of local pond and river life and set up a pond in the school ground. With the help of the teacher they began to see the need to keep a natural balance of living things in the pond; further work led to an understanding of the purification process in the school swimming pool.

Animals

2.128 The keeping of small animals such as rabbits, mice, guinea pigs and gerbils provided opportunities for learning their habits and how to care for them but there was little evidence of close and systematic observation and the animals were often taken for granted after a while; for example children seldom attempted a more detailed study of the needs of small animals or recorded weight, or variety of foods offered. In a number of instances small animals were treated as playthings and this is a matter for concern. On the other hand in a class of 8 year olds the children were using an incubator to hatch pheasant and bantam eggs. The development of the eggs, which were turned twice daily, was observed by holding them in front of an electric light, the temperature was controlled, and groups of children kept a daily diary recording the activity undertaken and the observations made. In some schools the children studied insects, fish and birds.

2.129 Some classes studied animals from other lands. A project with 9 year old children on 'Animals of the World' arose from a television programme on jungle animals. It required the use of a world map with the countries labelled; animals native to each country were drawn and descriptive accounts written. Other children became interested in camouflage, after a visit to the zoo; this also led on to map and atlas work and a study of the natural habitats of animals. Fossils have a particular interest for young children and were frequently brought into school by them, this often leading to interesting discussion and writing. One 7 year old child wrote

'Millions of years ago when a plant, tree, animal or fish died and fell on a piece of mud, lots of mud and rocks came on top of it. Then some water and minerals came and went into the bones of the animals and they turned to stone. Many years later a person came and dug it up and put it in a museum. It is called a fossil.'

Plants

2.130 Throughout the age range there was provision for the study of living things. Seasonal displays of wild and garden flowers, fruits and seeds, twigs, leaves, grasses and fungi were provided on the nature tables in most of the class rooms for 5 and 6 year olds. There were many instances of children growing things such as bulbs, mustard and cress, peas and beans. In addition to the classroom, halls and corridors frequently had displays of plants, leaves and flowers. In most cases the work arising was mainly descriptive and did not bring out scientific thinking.

2.131 However there were exceptions. For example, in one class an experiment was conducted on the germination of seeds. The children observed the effects upon growth when seeds were planted on blotting paper, cotton wool, soil or sand and with and without light, water and warmth. In another school observation of germinating seeds in a plastic bag led an 8 year old to write:

'It is a mini greenhouse; the coldness outside makes condensation and that waters it'.

6 year olds drew plants and flowers, including the pattern of fruits, from direct observation. Occasionally the paintings of trees, flowers and animals showed accuracy of detail, as when some children painted pictures of the pet rabbit and others made charcoal sketches of an owl. A group of older children carefully observed, drew and coloured wild roses, foxgloves and grasses which had been brought into the classroom. The school grounds offered further opportunities for studying living and growing things but good and positive educational use was made of them in very few schools and schools with particularly rich or exciting surroundings were not making any more use of them than schools in less favoured areas.

Farming and fishing

2.132 The children's interest in their local area often provided opportunities for careful observation and recording which enhanced their learning. A class of 5 year olds visited a local farm to observe milking time and there was a discussion about the size and age of the cows, their registration certificates, the milk and the milk products. On their return to school they painted pictures of milking time and making cheese. Before the children in a small rural school visited a local agricultural training centre they were given assignments which introduced them to scientific, geographical and mathematical information useful to them on the visit. The children made a survey of the animals, their food, and of animal products such as milk, wool and meat. They also studied the crops grown, the system of rotational planting and the eventual use of the crops and they examined the farm machinery. The preparation for and follow-up of the visit led to displays in the hall, relating, among other things, to the food of the cows and calves.

2.133 In one school the 8 and 9 year olds were preparing for a visit to a nearby fishing port to learn about deep sea fishing in the context of a local study. The visit was planned to include a tour of the harbour and the fish market, a visit to an ice factory and a guided tour aboard a deep sea trawler. Teacher and pupils were also planning to visit a maritime museum. Their effective preparatory work involved the extensive use of books, including reference books concerned with geography, science and mathematics.

Commentary

2.134 All of the schools provided some teaching that helped the children to understand the physical and natural world, leading in various degrees to the use of observational skills and to scientific thinking. Much of this work could with profit have been further developed.

2.135 With the younger age groups, although science seldom appeared as a subject on the timetable in all but a few of the classes visited work that might be identified as science was usually introduced incidentally. With the 6 year olds the work frequently took the form of weekly topics. From the age of 7 there was a more systematic provision for science and for the 8 and 9 year olds there was more likely to be a regular timetabled lesson which implied that science had a place in the curriculum.

2.136 Individual pieces of work were usually well planned but seldom linked in a way that ensured a gradual and steady growth of skills and understanding, though there was certainly some improvement in the accuracy of individual observations as the children became older. Practical work was too often done by the teacher but it frequently gave rise to enthusiastic discussion. The recording of what had been observed provided opportunities for children to write in their own words, but often their part was limited to copying from the blackboard or from books.

2.137 In some classes it appeared superficially that the children were receiving an education in science and that there was an experimental approach, yet on closer observation little real scientific work was being done. Both the rigidly timetabled approach and the incidental approach, which sometimes masked unplanned work, contained weaknesses. The former often gave rise to a series of isolated topics unrelated either to the children's current interests or to each other and which were followed up inadequately. The latter frequently lacked the essential basic planning needed to ensure adequate content and continuity, and depended on the skill of the teacher in recognising appropriate situations and developing their potentialities. Both approaches might be made to work if a clearly prepared scheme was used indicating what should or might be covered and the inter-relations between the various parts of the scheme.

2.138 In almost one-third of the schools the book provision for science was good. Reference books on natural history were often used on display tables. The book provision was frequently better than the programme it was intended to support. The youngest children generally fared worst for books.

ART AND CRAFT

2.139 Within the school the quality of the children's visual experiences and the work resulting from them depended as much on the skill shown by teachers in arranging the classrooms and the communal areas in ways that were functional yet reflected good standards, as on the teaching. More than a third of the schools were arranged in this way to stimulate the children's aesthetic awareness. In these schools the children's work, books, artefacts and natural materials such as wool and wood were displayed attractively. It was rare to find displays which included artefacts from other lands or which reflected art forms of different cultures in society. Overall the quality of the materials and the standard of display, the care and arrangement of the equipment and apparatus, and the general orderliness in the school contributed to the good aesthetic quality of the surroundings, which was not determined by the age or type of the school building.

2.140 The outdoor areas were being used positively to help foster aesthetic awareness in only 20 schools. In eight other schools they were sadly neglected; grass was uncut, flower beds were untended, apparatus was deteriorating, and little had been done either by the schools or the local education authority to plan and maintain areas that were interesting, attractive and aesthetically pleasing.

2.141 The time set aside for creative work varied considerably between age groups. On the whole the younger children had more opportunity for art and craft than older children in the same school. In approximately half the schools the younger children had a daily period often lasting for an hour, during which the children used art and craft materials or took part in social and dramatic activities. Some schools provided time daily, or almost daily, for art and craft for all age groups; others restricted this kind of activity to approximately an hour on one or two afternoons a week. In some cases the creative work was confined to a timetable period in a shared practical area, and this seriously limited the development of ideas and skills and tended to separate most of the art and craft from the rest of the curriculum. On some afternoons the children in a small number of schools were allowed to make a choice that included certain art and craft activities. In rare cases this was the only opportunity for art and craft, so that some children were never involved in this part of the curriculum. In some cases the older boys and girls were taught separately for art and craft. During the period of the inspection in one school the 7, 8 and 9 year old girls made gingham aprons while the boys made paper lampshades; in another school the 7 and 8 year old girls sewed on binca canvas and knitted while the boys painted and made drawings and collage pictures. There is no justification for practices such as these which differentiate the curriculum for boys and girls, and they should cease.

2.142 Art materials tended to be used almost exclusively to produce pictures. In addition to a variety of paper, pencils, paintbrushes and crayons were available in most classes, and many children also used felt tip pens and gummed paper. During the course of each day virtually all the children illustrated stories and other written and mathematical work. Many of the older children illustrated their topic work by copying pictures from reference books, though some of them were making considerable progress in drawing and painting from the careful observation of natural and man-made objects. Fabrics such as binca canvas, gingham and felt were used, particularly in the older classes of the 5 to 9 schools. Throughout the age range children had the opportunity to make pictures with a variety of materials that gave valuable experience of different textures.

2.143 The number of classes involved in three-dimensional work was comparatively small and a limited range of materials was offered. Modelling materials such as plasticine were used in many classes, particularly with the young children but clay was seldom available. Wood was rarely used by the children, even though the facilities and tools were available in a number of schools. Materials such as plaster, soap, polystyrene, string and cane were occasionally available. A good range and quality of materials resulted in good work. The children were usually given help in the safe and efficient handling of tools and they demonstrated skill in the use of them. Occasionally children were trying to use tools but where not given sufficient help in selecting or using the right tool for the work being undertaken. In a few classes the work of the older children was impressive, both in its variety and finish, and there were instances of the work enriching the curriculum as a whole as well as constituting an achievement in its own right. Some of the best work, particularly with older children, arose out of the application of art and craft to other areas of the curriculum such as the drawing of artefacts, plants and animals, and the work arising from museum visits. There were relatively few instances when children were given the opportunity to discuss what they had produced.

2.144 The educational value of some of the work was very slight when, for example, children were using crayons or tissue paper to fill in outlines drawn by the teacher, or were drawing around templates. Children sometimes modelled with materials that had lost their quality, for example with clay that was too dry, or with battered egg boxes. Some of the group work, class picture and model making was too prescribed and teacher directed. Even where children were introduced to a variety of techniques, the learning of the technique was sometimes taught in isolation and became the prime objective, instead of being used for a purpose. An example of this was where puppets had been made and displayed but were not otherwise used.

2.145 Elsewhere there was little evidence of progression and development in the use of materials and tools. There was little difference in the standards expected by teachers of children of different ages and ability. The use of a well thought out range of materials of quality usually resulted in a wider variety of good work. The range of activities for the younger children was usually wider than for the older children, but in a number of classes the full potential of the work was not realised because while the children were drawing, painting or modelling the teacher was busy helping children with work in the basic skills. Thus the educational value of art and craft work was often not realised.

Commentary

2.146 Almost half the schools were concerned with promoting aesthetic and sensitive visual and tactile awareness in the children and some teachers appreciated the educational value of the work in art and craft. The quantity and quality of materials for two-dimensional work was adequate, but there was a severe limitation of the range and quality of media available for modelling.

2.147 The work was of a high standard when the children had the opportunity to observe closely before they drew, painted or modelled; however there was a disappointing lack of progression in the work. As in every other area of the curriculum, it is unnecessary and unacceptable for boys and girls to be taught separately for art and craft.

MUSIC

2.148 Every school visited provided some singing for all pupils. In about a quarter of the schools the standard of singing was high, the children's musical ability well developed and the work was lively. The work with the 5 and 6 year olds included songs, nursery rhymes, jingles, action songs, singing games, finger plays and hymns. Sometimes the children accompanied their singing with percussion. With the older children the range of songs was sometimes impressive and included folk music, pop songs, modern and gospel lyrics. The use of radio and television programmes increased with the older age groups. Hymn singing and hymn practices played a significant part in the work of the majority of schools, although some of the sessions were excessively long. Choirs were organised in a number of the schools, sometimes for volunteers, sometimes by means of auditions. 8 and 9 year old children from one choir introduced new songs and hymns to the rest of the school at the weekly singing session for the whole school.

Instrumental work

2.149 The playing of tuned and untuned percussion instruments was taught in most schools to most pupils; this was sometimes used to accompany singing and on rare occasions to create sound pictures to illustrate a story. Often the instruments, some made by the children, were used as part of the recommended activities in school radio programmes. Music corners containing percussion instruments were available in a number of the 5 year old and some of the 6 year old classes but there was little evidence of music corners contributing to individual or group music making.

2.150 Learning to play recorders began, in a few schools, with children of 5 and 6 years. However, the majority of schools first offered the opportunity of playing to the 7, 8 and 9s, although sometimes only to selected children. Recorder playing often made the most positive contribution to the musical experiences of these older children. Some 8 and 9 year olds and occasionally 7 year olds took part in playing handbells, steel drums and melodicas. During the period of the survey some of the older children, often a selected group in the 5 to 9 schools, were able to learn to play the violin or 'cello. In a number of the 5 to 8 schools and in a few 5 to 9 schools guitar groups existed for the oldest children. In a few instances the standard of instrumental performance was high.

Listening to music

2.152 Most children had frequent opportunities to listen to music, often during assembly. Occasionally children listened to music as part of their class lessons and, in isolated cases, went on to write, draw or paint as a result. Most schools possessed a reasonable collection of records and tapes; in some schools it was excellent in range, quality and number. However, there was little discussion about the music heard and most children were given little help in the appreciation of music. In a few schools the children were introduced to various instruments of the orchestra through live performance. In one instance a girl from the nearby middle school aroused a great deal of interest when she showed the first school children how her clarinet was assembled and then played it to them. From there it was a short step to playing a record of part of Mozart's clarinet concerto.

Resources

2.152 Most of the schools had the necessary resources for music, including record players, tape and cassette recorders, pianos, recorders, tuned and untuned percussion instruments, television sets and radios, song books and records. In a few schools the resources were exceptionally good; frequently they were under used. A third of the schools had a room designated for music, generally an empty classroom which had been converted for this purpose and suitable either for whole classes or small groups. A small number of schools used the hall but the conflicting claims of other activities, for example physical education, drama and school meals, often created problems. In a few schools either there was no hall or it was used as a classroom.

Organisation and opportunities for music making

2.153 There was considerable regrouping of children of all ages for music. Often this was to enable the children to be taught by the 'specialist' who usually was also a general class teacher. In approximately three-quarters of the school classes were combined for such activities as singing and music and movement; this resulted in large groups, often with a wide age range, being taught together. Where there was a wide age range it was very difficult to choose songs that were suitable for all the age groups and to ensure that all the children were developing a full range of musical skills.

2.154 Occasions such as school concerts and festivals, carol services and local musical festivals provided the stimuli for more polished performances. However there were instances of children having few opportunities for singing, of unsuitable choices of songs and hymns and of poor quality singing.

2.155 In the schools where the heads and other teachers were interested in music and regarded it as an important element in the children's education, the standard of musicianship was high, the range of work considerable and the level of the children's work commendable. In these few schools music played an important part in the general life of the school forming an element in the assembly and a link with other schools and with the community; in addition it provided enjoyment and contributed to an atmosphere in which gifts could be shared.

2.156 In one school where music made a special contribution to the work the teachers believed that all children could respond to music to some degree. The teachers were greatly strengthened by the presence on the staff of a part-time music teacher who worked admirably in a specialist capacity, setting standards of musicianship and communicating enthusiasm. In addition to teaching children she supported other teachers as they taught music to their own classes. There was a music room with a wide range of instruments suitable for the age groups. The teaching had links with literature and some assemblies included good music illustrated by pictures and writing. By the final year in the school children read and composed music and played recorders. Two concerts were given by the pupils each year and children attended concerts arranged by the local Schools Music Association. Some 300 records were stored in the school by the local Young Philharmonic Society and were used with the first school children.

2.157 In approximately a fifth of the schools music played little part in the general life of the school, the time given to it was minimal — less than two lessons a week — musical experiences were extremely limited in range and poor in quality, and there was a general lack of enthusiasm, appreciation and enjoyment. It was also possible for one aspect of the work to be satisfactory or even good, but for other activities not to be developed. It was, regrettably, exceptional to find younger children singing, playing simple musical games and listening to music as a regular activity in their classroom or class base, in the same way that they listen to stories or join in dramatic play.

Commentary

2.158 All the schools provided some experience of music for the children, but the quality varied. Not surprisingly where there were teachers with expertise and enthusiasm children attained a high standard in music making and had opportunities to listen to a wide range of music. Assemblies provided highly appropriate occasions when children could listen to others, sing and make music with a variety of tuned and untuned instruments.

2.159 In many schools problems arose where children were brought together in larger groups sometimes so that they could be taught by a specialist. This meant that children of widely differing ages were taught together and the material was not always appropriate for all of them. Where a specialist is available thought should be given to the best use of this teacher's time and expertise. It may be more beneficial to use the teacher as a consultant; the other teachers could then have the benefit of advice and practical help so that they could teach their own classes.

PHYSICAL EDUCATION

2.160 With all age groups and in both 5 to 8 and 5 to 9 schools there were many examples of good physical education; the children were experiencing enjoyment and satisfaction from the varied activities, and enthusiasm was shown by children and staff. In a few cases high standards were found across all age groups in a school: the children were encouraged to extend and improve their own skills; bodily and spatial awareness were well developed: there was imaginative interpretation of themes; there was evidence of progression; and there was usually a daily lesson and a balanced programme of work including a variety of indoor and outdoor activities. 45 schools had guidelines and about half of these were supportive and helped the teachers to secure the development of appropriate skills and an effective continuity of content and standard.

2.161 There was evidence of some children being insufficiently challenged; they were unresponsive, sometimes lethargic, sometimes noisy and uncontrolled, and there was a lack of progression in the work. In schools where the teachers determined their own time allowance physical education was neglected. Some classes had only one or two lessons each week, for example, either for music and movement, or swimming or work on large apparatus. Schools with good resources did not always achieve good quality work. In a few schools, the amount of time allocated was substantial yet the range and quality of the children's work was poor.

2.162 Many classes of 5 and 6 year old children used the large apparatus and developed gymnastic skills, moved to music and worked with balls and small apparatus. Some learned to swim. Physical control was also practised and refined in connection with many parts of the curriculum during play with large toys, in art and craft, in drama and in writing. In most schools the provision for children from the age of 7 was greater in range than for the younger children. There were increased opportunities for games such as football and rounders, more work in gymnastics, more movement including dance, drama and country dancing, and more swimming. There was a concern on the part of the teachers that the 8 and 9 year olds should have opportunities equivalent to those of 8 and 9 year olds in junior schools. In many schools the range of activities for the oldest children was commendable.

2.163 In a very few schools no swimming took place. In four schools, particularly during the summer term, swimming was given priority and other areas of work lapsed. In some cases all the older children could swim on leaving the school. Interschool matches in, for example, football, occurred in some schools and involved the oldest children. In some of the small schools there were too few children to play full team games of this kind. There were instances even at the age of 7, but more frequently at the age of 8 and 9 years, when boys and girls were separated for games such as football, netball, cricket and rounders. There is no good reason why children should be separated at these ages. Sometimes children were allowed a choice of general activities and these included further opportunities for gymnastics, games and country dancing. Sometimes too these activities were supplemented by "clubs".

2.164 Most of the physical education took place in the hall. In approximately three-quarters of the schools the indoor space was satisfactory. The halls were usually of a good size and proportion with high ceilings, adequate ventilation and light and good floor surfaces which allowed work in bare feet; they were well maintained. In some schools long, narrow halls created problems; low ceilings limited certain key activities and restricted the height of the apparatus for the older children; arched ceilings were not suitable for hanging ropes. It was normal for the hall to be used for a variety of purposes; this sometimes severely restricted its availability for physical education. Nearly every school had a good supply of large agility apparatus, including climbing frames, benches, ladders, stools and ropes. In some schools the apparatus was unsuitable for the young children, and too heavy for them to move. For some of the oldest children the apparatus did not present sufficient challenge. Small apparatus, including balls, bats, ropes, hoops, quoits and bean bags was available in nearly every school and there was a good supply in over three-quarters of the schools.

2.165 Apart from games, not much physical education took place out of doors. In some schools outside work was confined to the summer term and in other schools it was not part of the programme. Although cold, snowy, weather during some of the survey visits prevented outside activities, full advantage was not always taken of fine weather.

2.166 The outdoor areas in about three-quarters of the schools offered good facilities for physical education and included both hard and grassed areas. In addition the outdoor provision sometimes included such things as fixed climbing apparatus, an adventure playground, a brick wall for ball practice, games pitches, playground markings and a swimming pool. Learner swimming pools were erected in some playgrounds; in others the pools were a permanent feature of the site. In a few schools the outdoor areas presented hazards; some were created by uneven surfaces, sloping ground and debris left when the areas were used after school hours. when children used nearby fields, public playing fields, parks and playgrounds, these offsite facilities were regarded by some staff as a bonus, but the distance from the school and the time spent travelling were seen by some teachers as deterrents.

Commentary

2.167 Every school in the survey undertook some form of physical activity, although the work was uneven in quality. There was little evidence of the progressive acquisition of skills. One factor which appeared to lead to work of high quality and progression was the presence of supportive and effective guidelines. Clearly another factor was the expertise of individual teachers.

2.168 The 8 and 9 year olds were not always sufficiently challenged, sometimes because of unsuitable apparatus, and sometimes because the work was an underestimation of the children's capabilities. There is no good reason why boys and girls should be separated for games.

3 The management of teaching arrangements and approaches

THE HEAD

3.1 A head is responsible for the ethos of a school. In the case of first schools the head's responsibility has been to create for this new age range an appropriate school community and to set for it reasonable standards. This implies, among other things and as for all schools, planning a suitable curriculum, establishing the organisation to implement it and a system for evaluating what is taught; it also implies maintaining good communications and relations with parents, the local community, the LEA and the heads and teachers of associated schools. The heads of the schools in the survey carried out these responsibilities in different ways depending on their personalities and convictions. No one way was superior to all others, but the 22 heads who were the more successful had managed in their various ways to establish good personal relations between the adults, teachers and others concerned with the schools; had created a sense of purpose and direction in the work and pride in what was achieved; and had used funds to purchase books and materials and equipment of good quality.

3.2 Most heads made sure that their teachers played a part in the fomulation of school policy. Many delegated responsibility for, at least, some areas of the curriculum to members of staff. Forty of the heads arranged that whole staffs met regularly on a formal basis, though at differing intervals, but 28 relied solely on informal gatherings at break or lunch times for staff meetings; often insufficient time was available for full and profitable discussion. The extent to which staff meetings were used for curricular planning was limited. In 12 of the schools planning was effective, attention had been given to ensuring a wide range of work, a balanced content, continuity and suitable stages of progression; in a further 11 schools a satisfactory degree of planning had been achieved.

3.3 As part of their policy for promoting staff development 18 heads helped and encouraged teachers to use and develop their special interests and expertise and there was a supportive attitude towards younger or less experienced teachers. In 8 of the schools teachers were encouraged to visit other schools. In half of the schools teachers had taken up in-service training opportunities provided by the

LEA or supported by it; some were encouraged by their head to apply their new knowledge and skills and to disseminate them among the staff.

3.4 In some schools heads worked alongside teachers in order to offer help and support and to provide training. This approach was not possible for the 12 heads who worked full-time with one class; it was not easy for the three who were in charge of a particular class for more than half the time. 21 of the others gave a high proportion of their time to working with small groups of children on a withdrawal basis, usually for reading. 16 of the heads taught some aspect of music and physical education. Their own example of teaching was thought by heads to be a profitable way to encourage and stimulate good practice among their staff.

PRODUCTION AND USE OF GUIDELINES

3.5   Nearly all the schools in the survey had guidelines for the work in English and mathematics. In all but 12 schools the agreed syllabus for religious education adopted by the local education authority was known, but less than a third of the schools were using it as a basis for work in this subject. Sixty schools had a guideline for religious education. Slightly more than half of the schools had guidelines for physical education. Guidelines for other parts of the curriculum were by no means so common; more than half of the schools had no guidelines for any other than the above subjects. The lack of guidelines for a subject did not necessarily mean that work in that subject was not covered.

3.6   Whether guidelines have any positive advantages will depend on the extent to which they go beyond a mere checklist of items to be taught. Good guidelines contain basic aims and specific objectives, clearly defined indicators of progression and detailed suggestions as to how the work might be developed. About a quarter of the guidelines for English, music and science, mathematics, physical education and art and craft fell into this category and evidence of their effectiveness may be deduced from the good quality of the work seen in the schools using them. In English the guidelines and schemes often referred only to the acquisition of basic reading skills. Approximately a third of the guidelines also gave some guidance for writing; spoken language was mentioned in a few schemes; there were very few references to literature, poetry or drama. In science the schemes that were of real use to the staff were those that gave help in selecting topics for study. In general the material covered by the science guidelines could be described as nature study although a few heads said that they were revising their schemes to include topics such as air, water, heat, magnetism and environmental studies.

3.7 There were instances of guidelines being written by individual teachers, usually where the teacher had responsibility for a particular part of the curriculum throughout the school; some resulted from the findings of a working group, either one within the school, or, more often, one organised on an area basis. In 77 instances an adviser had been involved in the devising of a guideline,[1] but by far the largest number, almost two-thirds of them, had been drawn up by the head, sometimes in consultation with another teacher or a group of teachers. There were 28 instances of guidelines being devised by the local education authorities mainly for religious education, as additions to the agreed syllabus, or for mathematics. Slightly more than one in six of all the guidelines produced by the schools were based entirely on commercially produced material; just over one-third relied partly on such material. These guidelines were mainly for language, mathematics and religious education.

3.8 There were many instances where guidelines were not used or were generally not supportive. Often they were simply lists of topics or activities and gave teachers little or no help in the planning of their work. In mathematics, about two-thirds of the schools had guidelines that were not supportive, sometimes because of the general nature of the statement and its lack of detail in indicating sequential stages, progression to be sought, practical experiences to be included and resources available. Fewer than half of the guidelines for language indicated possible stages of progression and even when there was a reference to this it was confined to progress through the reading scheme. The lack of well thought-out guidelines frequently resulted in topic work being developed on an *ad hoc* basis and the treatment of the subjects being superficial. Lack of an overall policy resulted in some schools in an unevenness in the quality of the work and lack of continuity and progression in both the content of the work and the standard reached; children covered some popular topics at the same level in different classes, or even in the same class if there was a wide age range.

CLASSROOM ORGANISATION AND TEACHING METHODS

3.9 Most teachers in the survey schools used a range of teaching approaches which varied to take account of the characteristics of the children, the resources available and the teachers' personal inclinations. Most employed a variety of teaching methods during the course of the week to suit the work in hand.

3.10 The teachers' own inclinations were strongly modified in 22 schools by policies which commonly reflected the views of the heads. In 13 of the schools the teachers followed a common school policy within which they had some freedom to choose their own classroom and teaching arrangements. However in 45 schools there was either no explicit policy or it was believed that each teacher should determine his or her own classroom organisation and approaches to

[1]Table 1, Appendix 2.

teaching. Some decisions should properly be in the hands of individual teachers but complete freedom of choice can be counterproductive. Extreme changes of practice from one teacher to the next are, at best, temporarily disconcerting for children and it is wise to adopt a framework of common practice. For example there should be common expectations about the ways children use learning resources and shared facilities and there should be an agreed system of record keeping.

3.11 Classroom organisation and methods were well suited to the children in all classes in 16 of the schools. In these schools there was a satisfactory balance between the opportunities provided for the children to find things out for themselves and more formal teaching. A good balance was kept between the activities initiated by the teacher and those chosen by children. Individual, group or class teaching was arranged according to what was being taught and the needs of the children, rather than from a belief that one arrangement was superior to the other. An aesthetically pleasing and intellectually challenging environment was provided so as to engage children's interest, evoke questions and stimulate discussion. Opportunities were made for children to experiment and be creative with a variety of materials. Work in the skills of literacy and numeracy was carefully ordered but at the same time children were required to make some choice of activity and given sufficient opportunities for imaginative, dramatic and aesthetic experiences. The teachers took reasonable account of the differences between children and followed up children's difficulties and mistakes. With the younger children play was sometimes used by the teacher as a basis for more directed work and with children of all ages their current interests were capitalised upon, when appropriate, to extend their learning. The work of the older children included tasks that required them to work collaboratively in groups, and they were made aware of the connection between what they were doing in for example, history, geography and science though these names did not necessarily appear ȯn timetables. In these schools the majority of children achieved satisfactory or better levels of performance across a wide range of their work.

3.12 In 35 of the schools such satisfactory arrangements and methods were practised in one or more of the classes, but in the other classes of these schools and in the classes of the remaining 29 schools the children's work was either over-directed to some degree or the children were given too little help in organising their work.

3.13 Where the work was over-directed, especially in reading, writing and mathematics, it was mainly restricted to repetitive practice in the skills when, in fact, children needed more experience in applying these in a variety of circumstances. The children had too few opportunities to exercise initiative and to raise questions. Schemes of work that made little allowance for differences in children's rates of progress were followed too slavishly; there was little evidence of the effective use of a combination of class work and individual or group work. The most common result, particularly in a small group of these schools where class teaching predominated, was that the more able children were doing work that was too easy for them but there were also a few examples of less able children, especially 8 or 9 year olds taught by teachers whose main experience had been with older children, trying to do work that was beyond them. Too little time was allowed for younger children to play with materials such as sand, water or building bricks, and even when time was given, the teacher did not extend the children's play towards further learning. Older children had no or few chances to investigate natural phenomena.

3.14 Where children were given too little help in organising their work the quality of what was done suffered to some extent because many worked too often as individuals rather than as members of a group or class. Individual work, when overdone, allows the teacher little time to discuss difficulties with the children in more than a superficial way and provides too few opportunities for the children to learn from each other. The work in these schools was characterised by a lack of accuracy and, in many cases, by too leisurely a pace. There was often little evidence of planning or record-keeping and children were seen working from cards or books in a random order.

3.15 Some teaching of the class as a whole took place in every survey school. The teacher brought the class together when he or she wished to give information, to tell or read a story or to read poetry, to share views and knowledge of events in "news" or discussion times, or to listen to music. When the children's interest was aroused and their imagination captured, the class experience offered a valuable means of learning, especially when supplemented by individual or group work. With the older children introductory work relating to historical, geographical or scientific topics was often appropriately taken with the whole class.

3.16 The balance achieved between individual, group and class teaching was particularly important in those classes which contained children of more than one age group. The teachers who used individual and small group teaching approaches in mixed age classes were more effective in establishing the confidence of the children and raising standards of work. However in about half the schools where the teachers were working with mixed age groups, two or three age groups in the class presented too great a problem. There were instances where the needs of the oldest, the youngest, the least able or the most able were not being met; this was due sometimes to an inappropriate programme. Sometimes the challenge of work did not match the ability or maturity of the children.

HOW THE TEACHERS WERE DEPLOYED

Class teaching

3.17 The relationship that a young child establishes with his teacher is an important one; it is often the first strong link that is made outside his immediate family. Most children starting school are helped by having one teacher with whom to relate and it is desirable, therefore, that teachers of young children should be responsible for all, or nearly all, of the day's work. This was arranged in almost all of the schools.

3.18 As the class teachers were teaching the children throughout most of the day, they had the opportunity, which nearly all took, to integrate the work and make links between the various areas of learning. To the extent that this occurred, fragmentation of the curriculum was avoided and the children were helped to make sense of the work. The class teachers generally knew the individual children well and understood the stage they had reached in their personal development and learning.

Teachers and consultants

3.19 Few teachers are expert in all parts of the curriculum. It becomes increasingly difficult for an individual teacher to provide the width and depth of all the work required to be taught to the older children and to cover a curriculum that requires, for example, more work in science, history and geography. The necessary help, support and advice may in part be given by heads and local advisers. It may also be provided by other teachers on the staff who have a special interest, enthusiasm and responsibility for a part of the curriculum and who act as consultants. Such teachers may give support in a variety of ways: by producing guidelines and schemes of work; by leading discussions and organising study groups; by disseminating work done on in-service courses; by working alongside class teachers; by assembling and organising resources; and occasionally by teaching classes other than their own.

3.20 In half of the survey schools a member of staff had responsibility for the work of the children in language, but in many instances this responsibility did not extend much beyond a concern with the provision of materials and resources.

3.21 In 30 of the schools, teachers, sometimes deputy heads, had overall curriculum responsibility for mathematics. In a few of these schools they were leading working groups on the production of guidelines, organising school-based courses for the staff and overseeing the work in mathematics in the school as a whole. In a few instances work of good quality could be directly attributed to the influences of the teacher "consultant"; for example, regular staff discussions had been held, support and help had been given to other teachers on choice of work, planning lessons and assessing children's learning. Too often, however, the role of the teacher with responsibility in this important part of the curriculum was limited to the production of guidelines or checklists or even, as with the equally important area of language, solely to the provision and organisation of teaching materials.

3.22 In just over half the schools a teacher had special responsibility for music. Occasionally, and most advantageously, the role comprised the range of support outlined in paragraph 3.19 and, in addition, responsibility for the school choir and instrumental group work. In other instances responsibility for music rarely meant more than playing the piano for classwork and assembly.

3.23 In only eight schools was there a teacher with special responsibility for the work in science. Good work in a class where the class teacher had little or no science was often the consequence of support exercised either directly in the classroom or indirectly through the class teacher by the teacher with special responsibility. Where help was lacking, teachers' diffidence about their own scientific capabilities too often resulted in their avoiding science, including nature study, and relying on a commercial scheme or providing charts and "nature tables" which were hardly used.

3.24 Details of the numbers of teachers with designated curricular responsibilities are shown in Table 8 in Appendix II.

THE ASSESSMENT, PLANNING AND RECORDING OF THE CHILDREN'S WORK

Assessment

3.25 A planned education requires the careful assessment of children's individual needs and the recording of their progress and development. As part of the day to day work of the classroom the teachers were continually assessing the progress made by individual children in order to decide, for example, when they were ready to learn a new mathematical process or to begin a new reading book. In addition to this about half the schools undertook more detailed assessments. In ten schools teachers made frequent and careful assessments of the children's abilities and attainments and consequent educational needs in most areas of the curriculum. Good systems of assessment were found in both large and small schools.

3.26 In a minority of the remaining schools some attempts at assessment had been made, but in most the importance of the more detailed assessment of individual children was not recognised. In such schools insufficient attention was paid to individual strengths and weaknesses, and in some cases only what a child was unable to achieve was noted. Attention was too often focussed on the requirements of the middle ability group in the class. Some teachers were successful in identifying and meeting the specific needs of the less able children but were much less aware of the capabilities and needs of the more able. A number of heads did not require teachers to make regular assessments; in others both subjective and more formal assessments led to a broad labelling of children merely as 'less able' or 'in need of remedial help'.

3.27 Generally schools that had good procedures for the assessment of individual children's needs, abilities and attainments were, not surprisingly, markedly more successful in providing appropriate work for their pupils than were those schools without such procedures. In reading and mathematics, the two areas in which assessment most frequently occurred, the work was usually better matched to the abilities of the average and less able children than to the more able. Overall, teachers tended to be more successful in providing suitable work in these two subjects than in most other parts of the curriculum.

Planning

3.28 In a few schools the assessment of individual children's needs was used in the planning of the next stage of work. There was evidence of this in adjustments to the planned range and content of the work, the formation of small teaching groups within the class, and the setting of appropriate tasks. However in the majority of schools little use was made of assessment. Frequently no adjustments were made to the previously planned class programme or assignment; there were instances where individual differences revealed by assessment were disregarded and teachers mainly used a class teaching approach irrespective of what was being taught. In some schools where individual teaching methods were being used the tasks set were too often inappropriate to the children's abilities. Sometimes very careful assessment was used only to plan the work for those children withdrawn from the classroom for special help. In a few schools poor forms of practice in assessment were found in classes which contained two or three age groups and teachers found it difficult to identify and meet the needs of the children at the extremes of the age and ability ranges, though not only because of lack of assessment.

3.29 Though few teachers took much account of formal assessment when taking decisions about subsequent work, the need for planning was generally recognised, and all teachers undertook some form of forward planning. The work in language and mathematics was more frequently planned than in the other subjects; slightly more than half of the teachers gave time to the long term planning of the work in these areas. A third of the teachers indicated that they planned the project or topic work. Though planning for work in other parts of the curriculum received some attention, references to such planning were much less frequent.

3.30 About half of the teachers described the general aims that were taken into account when planning future work. Their plans were made, for the most part, on a long term basis, half termly, termly, or yearly; this was also true of project work. The work in language and mathematics was the most likely to be planned on a weekly or daily basis. Very few teachers, only one in ten, mentioned discussing future work with their colleagues, or more rarely, with staff from the advisory or support services.

Record keeping

3.31 As part of their assessment procedures many teachers kept class records of the progress of individual children in one or more areas of the curriculum. Most schools had or were developing systems of record keeping in an effort to ensure greater continuity of learning. Records of children's progress in mathematics and language were kept by almost all schools; approximately half the schools, though not necessarily the same schools in each case, recorded progress in art and craft, in physical education, music and social development. Records of the children's progress in other parts of the curriculum were to be found in fewer than one-fifth of the schools.

3.32 The most commonly maintained records, those in language and mathematics, were almost always passed to the next class, usually in their complete form, but sometimes abbreviated to identify key stages of progression or particular strengths and weaknesses. Records of social development were passed to the next class a little less frequently, and usually in their complete form. Where records of performance in other parts of the curriculum or the results of intelligence tests were kept these too were usually passed to the children's next teacher. At transfer many of the records kept in the first schools were sent to the middle schools, though at this stage half the schools chose to abbreviate the information recorded before passing on the records. Sometimes information was transferred to local education authority record cards; occasionally these were supplemented by a selection of the children's work.

3.33 Part of the information included in the records was the result of tests administered in the first school. Testing procedures were used to confirm or supplement the teachers' own observations in almost all the schools; a variety of standardised objective tests were used, and some others personally devised by the teachers. Tests were used mainly to monitor progress, sometimes to identify learning difficulties and, in a very few schools, to assist in the planning of future work. In half the schools tests in language and mathematics were administered once during a child's time in the first school, and twice in a further quarter of the schools. Progress in English, mainly reading, was tested in all but one school, and almost half the schools used tests to assess progress in mathematics. Ten schools were required by their local education authorities to administer English tests and five schools administered other tests, including those for mathematics, for the same reason.

4   Summary and conclusions

4.1 The schools in the survey, whether 5 to 8 or 5 to 9, have characteristics which closely resemble those of other primary schools. They have established the same good relationships — both within the school community and outside it with parents and others — found in the primary schools looked at in the national survey. There are close similarities in the curriculum and the organisation and teaching approaches used to implement it; there are parallels in the children's work with what is done and the standards achieved. This was largely to be expected: the only difference from other primary schools shared by the schools inspected was their extended age range compared with infant schools, a difference thought to encourage greater security of learning for some children. It remains to ask what progress has been made towards that aim and whether 5 to 8 or 5 to 9 schools seem likely on present performance to be better placed to achieve it.

5 to 8 and 5 to 9 schools

4.2 There are marginal differences between these two kinds of first schools and between them and others with more traditional age ranges. The teachers and particularly the heads of the 5 to 9 schools in the survey were more inclined than those of 5 to 8 schools to differentiate between provision for the youngest and oldest children. One sign of this was the greater chance in 5 to 9 schools that one teacher had been given special responsibility for the younger children[1]. It might be, however, that the heads of the 5 to 8 schools, many of whom had been heads of infants schools, did not feel it necessary to delegate this responsibility.

4.3 A very few 5 to 8 schools have programmes for the 8 year olds that are reminiscent of practices in old-fashioned junior schools and are highly dependent on narrowly conceived exercises in English[2] and mathematics[3] and isolated lessons in geography and history[4]. Also a small minority of teachers of the oldest children in the 5 to 9 schools, perhaps remembering the work

---

[1]Table 10 Appendix II   [2]Paragraph 2.24
[3]Paragraph 2.67   [4]Paragraph 2.111

achieved by 11 year olds, had mistakenly concentrated the work on specific exercises and mental drill in such a way as to diminish their pupils' chances of developing initiative and the power to use skills they had acquired.

4.4 But it would be wrong to make much of these differences. They hardly existed in a good many of the schools and taken as a whole the work of the schools in the survey falls within the range of that of all schools that include children of these ages. A few offer a very good education indeed. A few are less than satisfactory either because they leave too much to chance or because what they offer is too superficial or too narrow for children today. Most fall between these extremes, exhibiting some strengths and some weaknesses but generally provide satisfactory foundation to most pupils' schooling.

4.5 The survey affords no support to the argument that first schools should revert to infant or junior with infant schools; nor does it lead to the view that their number should be increased. Other external factors may favour one or the other of these views. The effectiveness or cost of middle schools may have a bearing on the question. Falling rolls and the need to pay particular attention to the size of schools may lead local education authorities to decide that more effective primary and secondary education could be provided if there were changes in the ages at which children transfer from one phase of education to another; the introduction of sixth-form or tertiary colleges may have a backwash effect on first schools. But this survey does not contribute positively to the debate. It cannot be said that children in these schools, as they are at present, would have made more or less progress by the time they were 8 or 9 had the transfer age been different. Of course if the 5 to 8 schools reverted to infant schools and the 5 to 9 schools to junior with infant schools the morale of the teachers and so the work of the children might well be affected. Among responses to a question inviting heads to express their views on first schools in the light of their own experience there were indications that the morale of teachers in 5 to 8 schools would become worse and that of 5 to 9 teachers would improve.

Main outcomes

Personal and social development

4.6 The survey indicates that personal relations in first schools are very likely to be good and that children learn to behave well in school, to respect other children and adults, and to take care of property. Children develop self-confidence and assume responsibility for a variety of tasks in the school[1]. Such responsibilities are usually given to the oldest children even though the younger children might be equally capable. In infant schools it is the 7 year olds who are encouraged to assume responsibility and exercise leadership, but this practice is rarely found in first schools.

[1]Paragraphs 2.92, 2.93

Standards of work

4.7 Nearly all children make a satisfactory start in learning to read, write and calculate and most achieve a satisfactory level of attainment in the early language and mathematical skills; however, the development of these is more variable. Standards of performance in other parts of the curriculum show a similar variability. Rather more progress might have been expected of most children, particularly of the older and more able children. One reason for this gap between performance and potential is likely to be that teachers, rightly conscious of the importance of the skills associated with reading, writing and mathematics, allocate too much of the children's time to the practice of isolated examples and too little to the application of the skills in a variety of circumstances[1]. Even more important, the skills practised are sometimes not well-matched with the children's ability to use them. Another reason, but a far less frequent one, is that the order of work is not well worked out; this difficulty sometimes occurs when teachers try to provide different work for each child in the attempt to allow for fine differences between children. A similar finding is reported in the national primary survey.

4.8 It has always been difficult for the teacher of young children to achieve the right balance between hearing children read individually and working with small groups or the class. Regardless of the time it takes, many teachers are concerned to hear all or most children read each day. This practice, like others, can have disadvantages if it is engaged in unselectively. Some fluent readers need to be heard much less than daily; they show how well they are reading by what they do with their reading. Others do need to be heard frequently and for a reasonable period of time. Sometimes this is done when most children are painting or engaged in some other practical work. Care, however, has to be taken, that good educational opportunities for discussion, extending children's range of work, introducing new ideas, and setting children off on new and more demanding work arising from these activities are not lost because of the time taken in listening to children read.

4.9 In mathematics opportunities for the extension and application of mathematical skills are often limited by an over-concentration on the practice of such skills. Teachers devote much time to work with numbers and the practice of the four rules and many children achieve a satisfactory level of competence in this narrow field, but few have sufficient opportunity for learning how to apply the skills they acquire to the solving of problems. Practical work in measurement is undertaken in many schools. The mathematical experience of most children includes handling coins, accurately performing written calculations with money and work on shape. Too few schools make good use of the opportunities for the development and extension of mathematical understanding which arise in

---

[1]Paragraphs 2.4 and 2.76

children's play, in their interests and experience and in the work in other parts of the curriculum[1].

4.10 It is interesting to note that in contrast to the findings of the national primary survey there is more evidence in the first schools of work intended to help children to understand the physical and natural world and which might develop the children's skills of observation and lead to early scientific understanding. There remains a need for essential basic planning of the work to provide adequate content and continuity. Although individual topics and activities are often well planned they are seldom linked in a way that might lead to a growth of skills and understanding. Sometimes the work lacks depth; the potential for a scientific approach to an everyday event or experiment often remains unrealised because of inadequate preparation or suitable follow-up. There is often a lack of awareness of the appropriate skills or ideas which might be developed.

Children with special needs

4.11 Children with learning difficulties, particularly those associated with learning to read, are soon noticed and special teaching arrangements are usually made for them. Schools may rely entirely on their own resources or may call on the help of peripatetic teachers or educational psychologists. Sometimes, not necessarily because a child has difficulty with reading, psychiatric help may also be required. There are still too many cases where the help of the educational psychologist or psychiatrist is said to be not quickly available. There are also too many occasions when, after initial investigation and assessment, the teacher is not told what the findings are or, more often, not advised how to proceed.

4.12 Children with lesser degrees of difficulty do not need such specialised help. For these children it is especially important that a coordinated programme of work is arranged, that every suitable activity is made to contribute towards progress in reading and writing[1], and that the remedial teacher and class teacher work closely together.

4.13 The able children are rarely given extra help, yet they also may need close attention if they are to make the progress they should. When possible, arrangements need to be made to bring these children together from time to time so that they may benefit from mental stimulation and not feel as isolated as they sometimes do.

Ethnic minorities

4.14 All children should be made to feel members of the school community. This is as true where there are a few children from ethnic minority groups as where

---

[1]Paragraph 2.69, 2.70

there are many. These children may need additional help with English, and this is almost always provided[1], and in schools with substantial numbers of such pupils make take the form of a small group of children withdrawn from their class. They should also be made to feel that their cultural backgrounds and practices are valued in the school[2]. Indeed all schools, whether they include children from ethnic minorities or not, should prepare children for life in a multicultural society, and help representatives of each culture to appreciate what others can bring to the community.

The planning and assessment of work

4.15 There was plenty of evidence in the survey schools that good guidelines, although no guarantee of success in themselves, are a step on the way. More might be done, with the help of local authority subject and phase advisers, to extend the number of guidelines that are now being drawn up. They are now most numerous in mathematics and English, though the latter need to include more guidance in respect of spoken language[3]. They are urgently needed in all parts of the curriculum, and especially in geography, history and science. There is no reason why, as a result, these subjects should appear separately on the timetable, but these is need to identify the topics for study that are appropriate bearing in mind the locality and the skills and ideas that should be included.

4.16 In times of falling rolls more classes with mixed age groups will occur. This survey added to the evidence that mixed-age classes present difficulties for a substantial number of teachers. In this survey it was noticed that both the more and the less able within the class might suffer some neglect[4]. Where mixed age classes must occur thought needs to be given how to minimise some of the problems. It may be that ancillary or peripatetic help should be directed particularly to these classes, or that heads should give them more than an equal share of their own time. Attention should also be given to the in-service training needs of teachers who have such classes.

4.17 Mixed-age classes for the youngest children can have certain advantages. By this arrangement they may make it possible for new entrants to school to stay and settle in a class for a year or more.

4.18 Whether vertically grouped classes are arranged or not, it is important that young children have a reassuring and stimulating start to their schooling. It almost always proves useful to introduce children to school a few at a time, and heads who arranged staggered entries spoke favourably of the practice. The visits by HMI for this survey were seldom made at the beginning of terms, but many others of a different nature bear out the heads' views.

---

[1]Paragraph 2.39   [2]Paragraph 2.95
[3]Paragraph 3.5   [4]Paragraph 3.16

4.19 If children are brought into school at the beginning of the year in which they become 5 some are sure to be very immature on entry. Part-time schooling is as much as some of these children can reasonably manage at first. They need almost the kind of education they would get in a nursery class and that is not easy for a teacher to provide if there are 25 to 35 children in a class a good many of whom are under 5.

Responsibilities of heads and teachers

4.20 The survey, as did the survey of primary schools before it, shows the importance of good leadership in the school, not only from the head[2] but also from other members of staff each taking responsibility for an aspect of the work[3]. There is no doubt in the minds of those responsible for the survey that the quickest progress could be made if thorough training were made available for these teachers. It is also necessary to help the teachers to engage and lead others in their efforts, for if primary and first schools could ever have been operated by teachers working separately and pursuing their own inclinations, that day is past. Not only do the teachers need to work together, but teachers, ancillary workers, parents and the community need to understand and support the work of the whole school.

Implications for in-service and initial training

4.21 The evidence of the survey reveals a number of both in-service and initial training needs. The majority of teachers come from other than first schools, and these teachers need appropriate in-service training to help them translate the best schemes into good practice. For those heads who have accepted responsibility for an age range in which they lack training or experience, opportunities are required for increasing their knowledge of children at this stage of development, planning and organisation. Appropriate courses need to be offered so that teachers can, with expertise and confidence, accept the challenge offered by the admission into ordinary classes of children with a wider range of special needs. It is not reasonable to expect all teachers to have the necessary depth of knowledge and range of expertise across the whole curriculum; this is one reason why some division of responsibility is advantageous — though in first schools there is hardly any for the teaching. Further opportunities are needed for some teachers to extend their knowledge and gain additional skills in particular parts of the curriculum, and to study ways in which they can give effective support to other members of staff.

4.22 Those providing initial training courses should bear in mind the needs of first schools. For children in the age ranges 5 to 8 and 5 to 9, one teacher usually takes responsibility for the work of the class which means that the professional

---

[1]Appendix I, 2   [2]Paragraph 3.11   [3]Paragraph 3.3

element in initial training related to first schools should equip such students with the necessary skills, knowledge and insights to tackle this work across a broad range of the curriculum.

4.23 Given the nature of the teacher's task in first schools the content of professional courses needs to be considered very carefully. Because of the needs of the student to know something of the broad range of the curriculum, the choice of the main field of study in a BEd degree, or the subject of their first degree should reflect the professional nature of the total training. This may mean restricting the range of subjects in a first degree which gives access to training to teach young children. The amount of time spent on the main area of work in a BEd degree course needs to be justified by its contribution to the student's professional competence in the classroom. In some cases the main subject might evolve from an extension of the study of a professional course — involving the necessary academic rigour — for example the study of 'language'. Equally the professional course might evolve from the main study. This work could form the basis of the expertise required by 'consultants' at a later stage in their career.

Appendix 1 Characteristics of the schools

Buildings and school sites

1. 72 of the schools were in premises previously used for pupils of primary age. Nearly half had been built since 1950 but almost a quarter before 1900. More than a quarter had been remodelled or extended. Eight had been purpose-built as first schools. Three-quarters of the 80 schools provided accommodation that was at least satisfactory for the range of first school teaching and learning. Where it was not satisfactory there was sometimes insufficient space or it was so unsuitably arranged as to inhibit the work of school. School sites varied in area and outdoor facilities but nearly every school had hard surface play areas, over half had pleasantly arranged grassed areas and over a third had playing fields. At the time of the survey almost all of the schools were in good decorative order and well maintained.

Admission arrangements for pupils

2. Considerable variation was found in the age at which schools admitted children. Twelve schools encouraged parents to enrol their children at the beginning of the school year in which they reached the age of 5, and 42 admitted children one or two terms before they become 5. The rest admitted children at various times of the year including the term after which they became 5.

3. The great majority of schools gave some opportunity for children and parents to see the school at work before the children were admitted. In a minority of cases there was a well designed programme of visiting over a few weeks at the end of which the child, if deemed ready, joined in some suitable activity such as painting or listening to stories. Most schools admitted the new children on the first day of the chosen term, others staggered the entry over a week or more so that children could be settled a few at a time. In 32 schools some children were allowed to attend part-time, usually on a half day basis for a short period.

Organisation of pupils

4. Single age group classes, were found in all or a majority of classes in 46 of the

schools. 24 schools organised mixed-age classes as a matter of policy, though not necessarily throughout the school, nor for the same age groups. In other schools a few mixed-age classes were formed when year groups were of uneven numbers so that class sizes could be reasonably uniform; where mixed-age classes occurred they most often contained children from two age groups. In schools where there were two or more classes of the same year group it was rare to find examples of streaming according to children's abilities; classes of this type were usually for the older children.

5. At the time of the survey staffing levels allowed nearly all the schools to form small classes or groups which met at regular intervals. About two-thirds provided special teaching, particularly for children learning to read. Most of these children were over 7. Three schools had formed special classes — usually of less than 20 and mainly for children over 7 years — where the children received all their teaching. Children requiring to learn English as a second language were also taught in small groups. Very occasionally groups of older and more able children were formed for special teaching. In about three-quarters of the schools children with learning difficulties were withdrawn individually from their classes for special tuition and were taught by a teacher employed mainly for the purpose, either full or part-time, by a class teacher temporarily freed from her class, or, especially in 5 to 8 schools, by the head.

Teachers: qualifications and experience

6. Including the head but excluding the teachers in nursery classes and special units there were 657 teachers in the survey; slightly fewer than an eighth were employed part-time. The range of pupil: teacher ratios for 5 to 8 schools was 16:1 to 27.7:1 with a mean of 23.7:1 and, for 5 to 9 schools, 10.5:1 to 27.7:1 with a mean of 22.7:1 (Table 4 Appendix II). Only three of the 5 to 9 schools had pupil: teacher ratios better than 16.0:1. Differences in pupil: teacher ratios were partly due to the smallest schools being more favourably staffed, as in the case of these three, and partly due to differences in local education authority policies. The overall pupil: teacher ratio in English primary schools in 1979 was 23.1:1.

7. About 90 per cent of the teachers were women as compared with 75 per cent in all English primary schools. All the heads of the 5 to 8 survey schools were women; men held the headships of approximately half of the 5 to 9 schools. Two of the deputy heads of the 5 to 8 schools and nine of the 5 to 9 schools were men; nine small schools had no deputy head.

8. Tables 5 and 6 in Appendix II give information about the qualifications of teachers and about the age range of children with which they had gained their main teaching experience. Broadly they show that the vast majority of the 657, whether in post as head, deputy or class or other teacher, were nongraduates whose previous experience had been teaching children in the primary age range;

and that somewhat over half of them gained their main teaching experience with children mainly aged 5-7. 68 of the remaining teachers were graduates, 10 of whom had not had teacher training. Three of the teachers had no formal qualifications but were qualified by long experience. The teachers whose main experience had been outside the primary age-range, just over one-fifth of the total, included 30 from secondary schools and colleges of education or further education, 22 whose experience was fairly evenly divided across a wider than primary age range and 63 who were new to teaching.

9. 30 of the heads were in their first headships. The distribution of the other 50 with previous headship experience holds no surprises since it was frequently the case that the head of an infant school which was reorganised as a 5 to 8 first school or the head of a junior or junior with infants school which became a 5 to 9 first school, remained in post. 15 of the 33 heads of the 5 to 8 schools who had previous experience of headship had been heads of infant schools and 22 of the 32 heads of the 5 to 9 schools with previous experience of headship had been heads of junior or junior with infant schools (Table 5, Appendix II). That the experience of the heads of 5 to 9 schools was mainly with children of junior age is a reminder that many of these schools were reorganised from junior or junior with infant schools (see Table 7, Appendix II).

The responsibilities of teachers

10. Nearly all of the teachers held the traditional responsibility for all or nearly all the work of one class. Among these were 12 of the heads and all but two of the deputy heads; a further three heads were responsible for a class for more than half of each week. Other heads taught for part of the week; a fifth taught some aspects of music or physical education; some took small groups of children for special tuition. 11 heads taught alongside class teachers. In 12 of the schools there was team teaching in which two or more teachers combined their individual expertise to teach more than a single class, either by exchanging or combining classes, or by regrouping children in their classes.

11. Teachers paid above the basic scale usually, though not necessarily, carried responsibilities additional to class teaching. The distribution of the principal responsibilities by salary scale of all teachers in the survey schools is shown in Tables 9 and 10 of Appendix II. Individual teachers often carried several responsibilities and overall these were more likely to be connected with the organisation of the school and its resources than related to the curriculum. Where responsibility for particular curricular areas had been allocated, it was most often given for music or language, followed by mathematics, art and craft and physical education. Teachers with curricular responsibility were often responsible for choosing and organising teaching resources, sometimes for preparing guidelines and occasionally, particularly in music and physical education, for teaching classes other than their own[1]. Overseeing the library

---

[1]See also Paragraphs 2.168 and 3.11 to 3.16

received the highest priority among the organisational duties of teachers with special responsibilities and responsibility for the organisation of resources and audio-visual aids were also common. The 5 to 9 schools were more likely than 5 to 8 schools to have teachers with specific responsibilities connected with the reception age of children. Both groups of schools attached a degree of importance to the induction of new teachers. One school in each group had included the need of the very able in the duties set out for a Scale 3 post.

Additional teaching staff and support

12. In addition to their own teaching staff just under half of the schools had regular visits from teachers or from paid instructors who were concerned with aspects of music teaching, remedial reading and language work and the teaching of English as a second language. Help from local authority advisers was most often concerned with physical education, language and music, either through local courses or through the provision of peripatetic teachers.

Other support services

13. Some two-thirds of schools said that they were readily able to obtain advice from the medical, paramedical, social services and school psychological services when it was needed but some schools found support from the schools psychological service limited because of the heavy workload on its personnel. It was reported that in a few schools children referred to this service often had to wait for as long as 18 months for investigations to begin. Only 10 schools had experience of poor liaison with one or more of these services; some schools regretted the lack of information following investigation of problems.

14. Additionally, a quarter of the schools received regular help from members of other local education authority or health support services including health visitors and school nurses, specialist teachers of travellers' children, teachers of the deaf, counsellors and speech therapists. A few schools were concerned at the lack of such specialists, especially speech therapists.

Paid helpers and voluntary help from parents

15. In most of the schools paid ancillary assistance was available. This was usually shared by all the classes in the school though a greater proportion of the time available was given to the youngest children. These ancillaries assisted teachers over a wide range of non-teaching tasks, thus allowing the teachers to make more effective use of their time with their class for teaching purposes. In a few schools help came from students in training on a National Nursery Examination Board course.

16. Parents helped teachers during school time in nearly three-quarters of the schools in the total sample. The number of parents involved in each school ranged between two and more than 40 sometimes working on a rota system. Some worked regularly for as much as 5 hours a week, others gave about an hour whenever they were able. Parents helped with a similar range of tasks to those of the paid ancillary helper. Three schools actively discouraged parental involvement in the work of the school.

Other links with parents

17. 23 schools had formally constituted parent/teacher associations, the membership of some of which included friends of the school, whose aims usually expressed the intention of bringing about a closer co-operation between home, school and community for the benefit of the children, and whose main activity was usually fund-raising. A number of these associations was very supportive of the school. In a few schools, as well as for social purposes, the parents met to discuss educational, social or health topics. 16 schools with no formal parent/teacher association had benefited from fund-raising activities by parents.

18. In almost all schools there was an easy informality in the relationships between parents and staff: parents were seen to come readily into the school and were made to feel welcome. Most of the teachers had a considerable knowledge of the home circumstances, needs and problems of the children in their classes. Much of this was the result of frequent, often daily, contact with the mother, or another member of the family, particularly in the case of the youngest children.

19. In 26 schools the parents were able to discuss their children's progress at almost any time without prior appointments. A few schools expected parents to use only the time at the beginning or end of the school day for discussion. In nearly half of the schools parents were requested to use occasions arranged by the school or to make appointments if they wished to discuss their children's progress. In many schools parents were invited to assemblies, carol services, concerts, exhibitions of work, talks on informal social events.

20. Oral and written messages passed on by the children and messages sometimes posted on school notice boards were generally used for informing parents on school matters. Fewer than a quarter of the schools sent out newsletters or information sheets relating to such things as events and special arrangements. A few schools provided booklets which included, for example, a history of the school, information on organisation, the school fund, open days, and the governing body. Most of these pamphlets were well produced and extremely helpful to parents in providing essential information about the school.

Links with the local community

21. In six schools playgroups were accommodated in classrooms and in one

Appendix 2 Statistical tables and note

This appendix consists of ten tabulations of data collected from the survey. Tables 1 to 10 appear on pages 68 to 75. These are followed by note on the statistics starting on page 76.

Appendix 1 concluded

case in the old school house. A few schools were used by other community groups during school hours and a small number of premises were used out of the school hours.

22. At least a quarter of the schools had established links with individuals or groups in the locality. Most often, these were old age pensioners for whom entertainment and gifts were provided, but links were also made with handicapped children and children resident in community homes, as well as with members of village associations. Funds were collected for charitable organisations.

Table 1 Incidence of guidelines for particular areas of the curriculum and by whom they were devised*

	Number of schools in which there is a guideline for the subject			Those involved in the preparation of the guideline			
				LEA adviser	Headteacher	2 or more teachers in the school	Individual teacher
Language	75	10	40	6	68	28	16
Mathematics	78	11	37	17	62	36	17
Art and Craft	36	3	5	4	23	4	10
History	20	3	4	1	13	3	1
Geography	18	1	3	1	11	4	1
General interest studies	32	4	8	5	25	7	5
Health education	22	7	6	3	9	1	4
Science	31	4	10	3	15	3	8
Religious education	60	19	18	12	26	6	3
Music	33	1	7	7	18	5	10
Drama	12	0	3	2	7	0	3
Physical education	45	4	10	16	25	7	2
Others	19	3	6	0	12	5	4

*In some schools advisers, head teachers and other teachers may all have been involved in the preparation of guidelines, so the last four columns may add to more than the number shown in the first column.

Table 2   First schools in England in 1975 and 1979

	Total number of first schools in 48 LEAs	
	January 1975	January 1979
Age range:		
5–7	8	9
5–8	828	1,068
5–9	1,128	1,550
5–10	129	222
Total	2,093	2,849

Table 3   Number of first schools in England 1970-1981

1970	227
1971	507
1972	647
1973	1,131
1974	1,787
1975	2,093
1976	2,311
1977	2,556
1978	2,706
1979	2,849
1980	2,887
1981	2,918

Table 4   Pupil/teacher ratios (PTR)

PTR	5–8	5–9	All schools
14.3–	–	2	2
15.0–16.9	2	2	4
17.0–18.9	2	5	7
19.0–20.9	6	7	13
21.0–22.9	3	4	7
23.0–24.9	7	16	23
25.0–26.9	10	7	17
27.0+	3	4	7
Total	33	47	80

Table 5   Previous headship experience of the heads

Previous headship:	Heads of the 5 to 8 schools	Heads of the 5 to 9 schools	Totals
Nursery	1	1	2
Infant	15	6	21
First	1	3	4
Junior	–	3	3
JMI	1	19	20
None	15	15	30
Total	33	47	80

Table 6 Qualifications of the teachers

	In 5 to 8 schools			In 5 to 9 schools			In all schools			Total
	Heads	Deputy heads	Other teachers	Heads	Deputy heads	Other teachers	Heads	Deputy heads	Other teachers	
BEd degree	1	–	12	–	–	11	1	–	23	24
Other graduates with teacher training	2	1	19	2	2	8	4	3	27	34
Other graduates without teacher training	–	1	4	1	–	4	1	1	8	10
Non-graduates	30	31	208	44	37	236	74	68	444	586
Qualified by long experience	–	–	1	–	–	2	–	–	3	3
Total	33	33	244	47	39	261	80	72	505	657

Table 7 Main phase experience of teachers

Main Phase Experience:	In 5 to 8 Schools			In 5 to 9 Schools			In all schools			Total
	Heads	Deputy heads	Other teachers	Heads	Deputy heads	Other teachers	Heads	Deputy heads	Other teachers	
Nursery	1	–	5	–	–	1	1	–	6	7
Infant	28	28	154	12	14	120	40	42	274	356
First	1	1	3	–	1	1	1	2	4	7
Middle	–	–	9	–	–	15	–	–	24	24
Junior	3	4	25	30	21	64	33	25	89	147
Secondary	–	–	6	2	–	14	2	–	20	22
College of Ed/FE	–	–	4	–	–	3	–	–	7	7
No one phase was more than half of total experience	–	–	3	3	3	13	3	3	16	22
None	–	–	35	–	–	30	–	–	65	65
Total	33	33	244	47	39	261	80	72	505	657

Table 8 Previous designation of the sample schools

	5 to 8	5 to 9	All schools
Former infant	24	5	29
Former junior	–	5	5
Former JMI	5	32	37
Former junior girls and infants	–	1	1
Purpose built	4	4	8
Total	33	47	80

Table 9 The allocation of curricular responsibilities within the schools

Curricular Responsibility	5 to 8 schools					5 to 9 schools					All Schools
	DH	Sc 3	Sc 2	Sc 1	Total	DH	Sc 3	Sc 2	Sc 1	Total	
Art and craft	3	–	10	3	16	4	–	7	–	11	27
Drama	1	–	2	–	3	–	1	2	1	4	7
General studies	2	2	4	–	8	3	–	3	–	6	14
Health education	–	–	–	–	–	–	–	2	–	2	2
Language	5	4	13	–	22	2	–	14	3	19	41
Mathematics	10	4	5	–	19	5	2	4	–	11	30
Music	1	1	14	3	19	7	2	11	3	23	42
Physical education	2	2	6	2	12	1	2	5	1	9	21
Religious education	1	–	–	–	1	–	–	1	–	1	2
Science	1	–	1	1	3	–	2	2	1	5	8
Other	1	2	18	1	22	6	–	13	7	26	48
Totals	27	15	73	10	125	28	9	64	16	117	242*
Total No of Teachers	33	13	121	110	277	39	16	97	148	300	577*

*80 headteachers and their responsibilities are excluded from this table.

Table 10 The allocation of organisational responsibilities within the schools * (80 Heads not included)

Organisational duty:	5 to 8 Schools					5 to 9 Schools					All Schools
	DH	Sc 3	Sc 2	Sc 1	Total	DH	Sc 3	Sc 2	Sc 1	Total	
Audio visual aids	5	–	12	–	17	3	–	7	1	11	28
Home/school liaison	4	1	5	3	13	–	–	4	1	5	18
Liaison with other schools	4	3	1	–	8	5	1	7	–	13	21
Library	7	4	14	2	27	4	5	19	2	30	57
Needs of the very able	–	1	–	–	1	–	1	–	–	1	2
New teachers	7	1	8	–	16	7	3	3	–	13	29
Nursery	–	–	1	–	1	–	–	–	1	1	2
Reception	3	1	7	5	16	2	2	16	10	30	46
Remedial	1	–	4	5	10	1	–	1	19	21	31
Resources	2	–	5	–	7	2	2	5	–	9	16
Supervision of students	3	–	1	–	4	3	1	6	1	11	15
Team leader	3	4	8	–	15	6	2	3	–	11	26
Year leader	4	2	8	–	14	1	1	6	2	10	24
Other	10	–	17	4	31	11	4	24	8	47	78
Totals	53	17	91	19	180	45	22	101	45	213	393*
Total number of teachers	33	13	121	110	277	39	16	97	148	300	577*

*80 Head teachers and their responsibilities are excluded from this table.

NOTE ON THE STATISTICS

Many proportions and figures are quoted in the Report. They accurately reflect what was found in the sample of 80 schools, but must be interpreted with some caution as indicators of what might be found in all first schools in England.

The survey is based on a random sample of 80 schools. Any random sample will be atypical in many respects. The atypicality of some characteristics can be controlled in the design of the sample and the bias of others, due to sampling, can be assessed on completion of the survey. However, for most characteristics there is no possibility of detecting whatever biases there might be; each proportion or figure is subject to an unknown sampling error. The only statement that can be made about a sampling error is that it is likely to be within theoretically calculated limits; for a sample of 80 schools these limits are quite large.

The design of the sample

In recent years, 5 to 8 and 5 to 9 schools have accounted for over 90 per cent of all first schools (Table 2). The survey was confined to these two major types of school. Two characteristics were controlled in the design of the sample. First the number of schools of each type in the sample was in proportion to the number of such schools in the national population at 1 January 1975. This date was chosen so that when the survey began in April 1978, no school that had been in existence for less than three years would be included in the sample. Thus a certain degree of maturity could be assumed. Additionally, within each local education authority, schools were selected in proportion to the number of first schools in that authority. So, for example, Surrey, which had more first schools than any other authority at that date, was represented in the sample by seven schools, a little over 4 per cent of the total for this Authority. At the other extreme, a few authorities with fewer than twelve schools were not represented in the sample.

The overall balance between the two types of school, 33 catering for 5 to 8 years and 47 for 5 to 9 years, was in proportion to the balance in the national population in 1975. The balance had changed very little by 1981.

Comparison of other characteristics with national statistics

In the sample it was not possible to control more characteristics than the LEA and the age range of the schools.

The incidence of two important but uncontrolled characteristics, the size of schools and their pupil/teacher ratios, can be compared with known national statistics. The comparisons are shown in Tables A and B opposite. In each case the right-hand column shows the number of schools of each size or PTR band that would have figured in the sample if it had been possible to control these factors. The left-hand columns show the actual numbers of schools in each band that made up the sample.

Two biases are evident. Medium-sized schools are overrepresented at the expense of both large and small schools; the pupil/teacher ratios of the sample schools are, on average, higher than those of first schools, nationally. Both of these biases are well within the theoretical limits of sampling error, but they are not without some significance should there be an attempt to relate the findings in the survey schools to all first schools in England. They serve, moreover, to illustrate the extent to which biases due to sampling may be present in other characteristics.

Sampling errors for other characteristics

For all other characteristics, for which there are no known national statistics, the sampling errors can only be placed, with 90 per cent confidence, within the ranges shown in Table C overleaf.

TABLE A   Schools

	Sample	Expected number
Number of pupils on roll:		
100 or fewer	16	19
101 — 200	34	25
201 — 300	23	23
301+	7	13
all schools	80	80

TABLE B   Schools

	Sample	Expected number
Pupil/teacher ratio:		
less than 20.0:1	17	20
20.0-24.9:1	39	42
25.0:1 or more	24	18
all schools	80	80

TABLE C

90 per cent confidence

90 per cent confidence limits for:

Percentages of a characteristic found in the sample:	Percentages of 33 5-8 schools ±	Percentages of 47 5-9 schools ±	Percentages of 80 first schools ±	Percentages of all teachers in the sample ±
5	5	5	4	2
10	9	7	5	2
**15	10	9	7	**3
20	12	10	7	3
30	13	11	8	3
40	14	12	9	3
50	14	12	9	4
60	14	12	9	3
*70	13	*11	8	3
80	12	10	7	3
85	10	9	7	3
90	9	7	5	2
95	5	5	4	2

*If the particular characteristic is found in 70 per cent of the 47 5 to 9 schools then the true percentage in the national population is likely to be within a range of 11 per cent on either side of the 70 per cent, that is the true percentage is likely to be between 59 per cent and 81 per cent. There is a one in ten chance that the true percentage would be outside this range.

** The limits are less wide when applied to the characteristics of all teachers. If a particular characteristic is displayed by 15 per cent of all teachers in the sample then the true percentage in the national population is likely to be within a range of 3 per cent on either side of the 15 per cent, that is the true percentage is likely to be between 12 per cent and 18 per cent. Again there is a one in ten chance that the true percentage would be outside this range.

Index

Printed in England for Her Majesty's Stationery Office
by Robendene Ltd, Amersham, Bucks.
Dd 717180   C100   5/82